THE
SAUSAGE
BOOK

THE SAUSAGE BOOK

The complete guide to making,
cooking & eating sausages

Nick Sandler & Johnny Acton

Photography by Cristian Barnett

Kyle Books

Published in 2011 by Kyle Books
www.kylebooks.com

Distributed by National Book Network
4501 Forbes Blvd., Suite 200
Lanham, MD 20706
Phone: (800) 462-6420; Fax: (301) 429-5746
custserv@nbnbooks.com

First published in Great Britain in 2010 by Kyle Cathie Ltd

ISBN 978-1-906868-34-5

Nick Sandler and Johnny Acton are hereby identified as the authors
of this work in accordance with Section 77 of the Copyright,
Designs and Patents Act 1988.

Text © 2010 Nick Sandler and Johnny Acton
Photographs © 2010 Cristian Barnett
Book design © 2010 Kyle Books

Project editor: Jenny Wheatley
Copy editor: Salima Hirani
Photographer: Cristian Barnett
Designer: Georgia Vaux
Food stylist: Linda Tubby
Props stylist: Liz Belton
Production: Gemma John

Library of Congress Control Number: 2011926475

Acknowledgments

The authors would like to thank:

Michael and Joan Little for rent-free use of their pig sties,
Angelina Harrison for corn dog inspiration, Weschenfelder
& Sons for essential sausage making equipment, Grassmere
Farm for pork supplies, Linda Tubby (the best food stylist
in the business), Bocaddon Farm for high-quality veal, Tim
Wilson and his staff at The Ginger Pig farms in Yorkshire,
Bod Webster and the Chapolard family in the Lot et
Garonne, Gref-Völsings in Frankfurt, Casa Riera Ordeix in
Catalunya, Jo McSween in Edinburgh, and our long-suffering
wives Lai and Percy. Johnny would not like to thank the
mailman who plonked a bunch of mail into the improvized
smoker in front of his house despite it belching smoke at
the time.

Websites offering sausage-related products:

www.scobiesdirect.com
www.weschenfelder.co.uk
www.designasausage.com
www.sausagemaking.org
www.sausagemaker.com

Nick Sandler is the Creative Chef for Pret A Manger,
and therefore responsible for countless lunches on a daily
basis. He is also a freelance development chef, creating new
dishes for delis and supermarkets.

Johnny Acton is a writer and amateur pig keeper who
has authored books on topics ranging from the role of high
altitude ballooning in the Space Race (*The Man Who Touched
the Sky*) to economics for kids (*DK Economy*).

Together Nick and Johnny have written five books for
Kyle Books—*Soup, Mushroom, Preserved, Duchy Originals
Cookbook,* and *The Branded Cookbook.*

CONTENTS

THE JOY OF SAUSAGES

The world, it is fair to say, is in love with the sausage. For large swathes of the Earth's population, life without hot dogs, chorizos, and salamis is scarcely imaginable. The Chinese would be miserable without their lap cheong, Germany boasts over 1,200 varieties of sausage, and even the Inuit get in on the act, inserting pieces of whale blubber into sections of intestine and air-drying or smoking the resultant packages.

So what is it about sausages that appeals to us so deeply? Well for one thing, people have been making them for millennia. Hunter-gatherers, whose lifestyle approximates to that of our distant ancestors, often chop up parts of their kills and roast them in the animals' stomachs (the original haggis). Sausages are mentioned in Homer's *Odyssey* and were so closely associated with riotous Roman fertility festivals that the Christian authorities banned them for six centuries. They might as well not have bothered, of course—Italians would no more give up their sausage than pasta— but the fact the Catholic Church even tried is a testament to the power of the sausage.

Tradition is clearly an important part of our devotion to sausages. They are also highly convenient fresh, easy-to-cook ones, and cured or smoked ones with long shelf lives. But the ultimate attraction of chopped ingredients stuffed into edible casings must lie in the things themselves. Freud would have a few theories about that, but for our money it's all about taste. The processes of sausage making allow tastes to be melded in unique and harmonious ways, while the casings form barriers that permit fascinating transformations to take place beneath, and also keep the contents succulent.

We could and will go on all day about the wonders of sausages, but a couple more of their advantages deserve special mention. First, they are economical. Sausages allow you to prepare delicious meals without breaking the bank. Even top-quality examples (the only kind we'd advise you to buy) are eminently affordable compared with conventional cuts of meat. Second, being almost universal, sausages offer an excellent and nonthreatening way to explore the world's diverse tastes and culinary traditions. If you get the sausage bug, you will never run out of new avenues to explore.

HISTORY OF THE SAUSAGE

Attempting to pinpoint the origin of something as universal as the sausage is a losing battle, but we can certainly trace the trajectory of its history in the West. The earliest written instructions for sausage making were etched onto a clay tablet in Sumeria around 5,000 years ago. The most significant sausage enthusiasts of the ancient world, however, were the Romans, who brought the art of stuffing ground meat into casings to every corner of their vast empire. They also provided many European languages with their vocabulary for the delicacies: the words sausage, *salsiccia* (Italian), *saucisson* (French), and *salsichon* (Spanish) are all derived from the Latin *salsisium,* which literally means "something salted."

As this etymology implies, sausage making prior to the modern era was primarily about meat preservation (salt is a powerful preservative that works by depriving foods of moisture, thereby impeding the growth of harmful bacteria). This was extremely important prior to the advent of refrigeration. It is easy to imagine Roman legionnaires sustaining themselves in far-flung parts of the empire by munching on primitive salamis and pepperonis. But the addition of salt wasn't the only way to give sausages long shelf lives. They could be dried, smoked, infused with antibacterial herbs and spices, or any combination of these techniques.

The methods of sausage production that became prevalent in any European region depended on its geography and climate. Around the Mediterranean, conditions favored the production of air-dried sausages, particularly in winter when the weather wasn't too hot. In the damper environments of Northern and Eastern Europe, "keeping" sausages were typically smoked to provide additional insurance against spoilage. Meanwhile, in every area, sausages were flavored with locally popular herbs and spices, such as caraway in Germany, ground pimento in Spain, and fennel seed in Italy.

Fresh sausages have existed for at least as long as cured ones, but in many areas they were less important economically because of the preservation imperative. As they needed to be consumed almost immediately after being made, fresh sausages were considered luxury items in preindustrial Europe. In line with their short shelf life, they often contained perishable ingredients such as eggs and cream, as well as highly expensive ones such as saffron and nutmeg. A good example of a medieval-style fresh sausage is the French boudin blanc (see page 22). Fresh sausages have always been the most popular kind in Britain, where cured and smoked varieties have never made much headway, possibly due to the excellence of the local ham and bacon.

The most significant developments in the world of sausages in the last 500 years have been, first, the transportation of traditional European recipes to the Americas and other former colonies and, second, the Industrial Revolution. Mechanization has transformed the production of sausages, often to the detriment of their quality. But in recent years there has been something of a backlash. More and more people are making their own sausages, whether out of ethical concerns about mass production, growing culinary sophistication, or both. A sausage renaissance is underway!

THE ULTIMATE SAUSAGE EXPERIENCE

Few things are as good as a good sausage, but the reverse is also true. Most people have had a ghastly sausage experience, be it an undercooked banger at a cookout or a revolting casserole at school. Unfortunately, the very nature of sausages makes it tempting for big businesses to "bury" substandard ingredients in them. They are frequently made with poor-quality meat from animals raised in distressing conditions and the practice of bulking them up by injecting them with water has become routine. "That's okay; it's all mashed up together so no one will notice the difference," some commercial producers tell themselves. Anyone who has eaten top-quality sausages knows otherwise. There are essentially two ways of ensuring that's what you get. You can either buy them from reputable suppliers or you can make them yourself.

Great sausages are packages of goodness made with top-quality ingredients. In our opinion, the best examples are those in which the contrast between the outside and the inside is maximized. Nothing can beat a freshly cooked sausage with a crunchy, caramelized exterior and a juicy, fragrant interior, unless it's a carefully fermented variety with a dry skin and meltingly soft contents.

TYPES OF SAUSAGE

There are various ways of classifying sausages but, for the purposes of this book, we've grouped them into the following categories:

Fresh sausages Neither cooked nor cured during the manufacturing process, fresh sausages need to be cooked and consumed within a few days of being made (alternatively, you can store them in the freezer for three to six months). They contain few preservatives other than salt, which is primarily present as a flavor enhancer. Fresh sausages are usually fried or grilled. Classic British bangers like the Cumberland (see page 16) and the Lincolnshire fall into this category, as do continental varieties such as the Toulouse (see page 17).

Precooked sausages As the name implies, sausages in this group are cooked or partially cooked as part of the making process. This is usually done either by blanching them in very hot water, as with Boudin Blanc (see page 22), or by hot smoking them, as with Polish Wiejska (see page 25). Most varieties of precooked sausages need to be heated again before they are eaten. Typical examples include Frankfurters (see page 24) and Saveloys (see page 25).

Cured sausages This is the category into which the likes of Salami (see page 21) and some kinds of Chorizo (see pages 18–19) fall. They are designed to be eaten raw, but also make excellent cooking ingredients. Cured sausages need to be matured over several weeks or months in a cool, fairly humid environment before they are eaten. During this period, a process of fermentation occurs. Curing is all about arranging things so that "good" bacteria thrive while the growth of "bad" bacteria is inhibited. The chief weapons in this battle are salt, temperature and humidity control, and, sometimes, the use of starter cultures. Cured sausages are designed for keeping—in other words, they can be consumed over a period of several weeks without significant deterioration.

Skinless sausages and sausage meat Sausage mixes that would normally be filled into casings can make excellent cooking ingredients. They can be formed into patties, meatballs, or dumplings, or used as beautifully moist stuffing.

Sausage cousins Haggis, black pudding, and the like are definitely part of the sausage family, but are distinctive enough to form a clan of their own.

Fish and veggie sausages This self-explanatory category demonstrates that sausage eating is far from a no-go area for nonmeat-eaters.

HOW THE BOOK WORKS

The Sausage Book is based on the assumption that you may or may not want to make your own sausages, but you'll certainly want to make sausage-based recipes. In this chapter, we show you in detail how to make a representative sausage of each of the three main kinds (fresh, precooked, and cured), followed by brief instructions on making other sausages within those families, including many that appear in our recipes. If you don't wish to make your own sausages, skip straight to the recipes. As well as showing you how to make your own sausages and some of the delicious dishes you can create with them, for inspiration we've included a number of features on superior artisan sausage makers—these are some of the best producers in the world. (Our only regret is that we couldn't make it to Italy, the home of many of the planet's finest sausages. The blame lies with the Icelandic volcano.) There is also a feature on Johnny's experience of keeping pigs—an often overlooked but important and rewarding part of the sausage-making process. We conclude with an A–Z of the world's sausages that, though far from comprehensive, we hope will further whet your appetite.

MAKING YOUR OWN SAUSAGES

You don't need to make your own sausages to enjoy our recipes, but if you do, it will increase your appreciation of them immeasurably. Sausages are among the most satisfying items to make at home. The process is great hands-on fun and the feeling of achievement that comes with producing a perfectly matured, top-quality salami or chorizo is tremendous. You never know quite what's in "supermarket" sausages—they often contain artificial preservatives and may be bulked up with water and other tasteless fillers. They also may not have been given enough time to mature properly. If you make your own sausages, none of this need apply. And you don't have to put up with the preferences of Mr. and Mrs. Average. If you like your chorizo extra spicy, just make it that way.

EQUIPMENT AND HYGIENE

Hygiene is always important in food preparation and is absolutely vital when making sausages. Grinding meat greatly increases its surface area and therefore its vulnerability to bacterial infection. The consequences of this happening to fresh sausages are bad enough; with cured ones, they can be catastrophic. Keep your hands and equipment scrupulously clean.

As far as equipment goes, the home sausage maker needs the following:

Grinder Ideally, this would have three plate sizes: fine, medium, and coarse. Some grinders double up as sausage stuffers, which saves you from having to buy one of each piece of equipment.

Sausage stuffer You fill the cylinder with sausage meat, then lower the plunger, which extrudes the mixture through a tube into the sausage casing. Manually-operated stuffers offer more control than electric ones. Choose a robust model with no crannies in which sausage meat can lodge and fester.

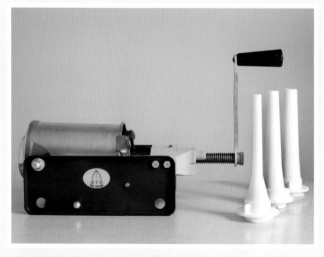  

Tubes Usually made of plastic, tubes are used to get fillings into their casings. They attach to your grinder or sausage stuffer (with which they may be supplied) and are available in various gauges in line with the varying diameters of different sausage casings. We'd recommend you to buy three: a narrow one for chipolatas, a medium-size one for average-size sausages, and a big one for salamis and chorizos.

Accurate kitchen scales Sausage-making ingredients need to be precisely weighed, especially curing salt and starter cultures. Choose a digital model that weighs in ounces.

Casings (skins) You can choose between natural casings (made from animal intestines), artificial but animal-derived ones (made from collagen), and cellulose ones (suitable for vegetarians). The last two types are not suitable for frying. Casings are available in a range of widths. Beef casings are wider than hog ones, which are wider than sheep casings. Your choice of tube should reflect the casings you are using. Buy casings from good butchers or online. Some suppliers wind them around spools, which makes life easier but adds to the cost. Others tie little plastic rings around the ends to help you locate them. When using natural casings, rinse them thoroughly of salt (they are packed in it to help preserve them) and soak them in tepid water for about an hour before stuffing them.

Disposable latex gloves Wear these when handling sausage meat, for hygiene purposes.

Butcher twine Use this to tie off the ends of stuffed casings.

Sterilized pin or needle You will need this for piercing stuffed casings in order to remove air pockets inside the sausages.

If you plan on making cured sausages, you will also need:

Maturing chamber Unless you're prepared to spend a fortune, you'll have to use your ingenuity here. You need to create an environment in which the temperature is maintained at 50 to 59°F, and the humidity, at 70 to 80 percent. You also need some air circulation. Nick uses an old refrigerator set to 53.5°F with a bucket of salt water inside to moisten the atmosphere. Johnny has a cellar with roughly the right conditions, and is able to fine-tune them by opening and closing the door and using a greenhouse heater. For more tips on making a maturing chamber, type "Creating an Ideal Environment for Dry Curing Sausage" into a search engine and follow the links.

Hygrometer and thermometer Use the former to check that the relative humidity within the chamber is at the required level, and the latter to ensure the temperature inside the maturing chamber is within the desirable range.

Starter culture A starter culture ensures that desirable lactic-acid producing bacteria immediately get the better of their harmful relatives in a sausage mix. Buy them from www.sausagemaker.com.

Curing salts Curing salts can be purchased online (such as www.mortonsalt.com) or at butcher's supply stores. They contain regular salt and sodium nitrite, which inhibits pathogenic bacteria, keeps meat from turning gray, and imparts a cured flavor. Some also include sodium nitrate (saltpeter), which gradually breaks down into sodium nitrite. These substances are dangerous if ingested to excess, so don't try mixing your own curing salt unless you really know what you are doing.

HOW TO MAKE FRESH SAUSAGES

Whether you're making fresh sausages for immediate consumption or varieties such as salamis that need to be matured over several weeks, the fundamentals of the process are the same. You need to prepare your ingredients carefully, then get them safely stuffed into appropriate casings. The photographs below show how to make a simple French paysanne-style sausage, consisting of coarsely ground pork plus a few herbs.

PAYSANNE SAUSAGES

Traditional fresh sausage recipes call for salt to form 2 percent of the total weight. We have reduced this to 1½ percent, as it's healthier and doesn't adversely affect the flavor.

Makes about 20 sausages

- 3 pounds 5 ounces pork (picnic) shoulder, cut into chunks
- 1 pound 2 ounces pork fatback, trimmed of all skin, cut into chunks (NB Instead of the 2 ingredients above you could use 4½ pounds fatty pork belly, trimmed of skin and bone and cut into chunks)
- 0.5 ounce fresh thyme, finely chopped
- 1 ounce flat-leaf parsley, coarsely chopped
- 1 ounce fine or flaky sea salt
- 0.4 ounce freshly ground black pepper
- 0.7 ounce garlic, chopped
- approx. 3⅓-yard length of spooled hog casings, soaked in warm water prior to usage

Before you start, make sure your surfaces and equipment are scrupulously clean. You may also want to wear a pair of latex gloves.

The process begins with grinding the meat (**1**) to the desired texture, which in this case is on the rough side (use a ¼-inch plate). Make sure you keep the meat cold throughout. This isn't just a matter of hygiene—if you allow sausage meat to warm up, it turns into unmanageable glue.

The next stage is to chop up the herbs and add them to the ground meat with the requisite quantity of salt (**2**). You then mix the ingredients by hand until they are evenly distributed.

Now comes the slightly suggestive business of rolling the casing onto the tube. With any luck, one end of the casing will be wrapped around a telltale plastic ring. If it isn't, you just have to scrabble around until you find an end. Once you have succeeded, slip the end over the tip of the tube (**3**), and gradually roll the whole casing onto it, bar a couple of inches. Then tie a knot in the projecting portion. At this point, you need to load your sausage stuffer with the meat-and-herb-mixture (**4**). Then screw the tube on and prepare to stuff. This will be much easier if you enlist the help of a friend. One of you turns the handle of the stuffer while the other controls the release of the casing (**5**). This is done by gripping the part of it nearest to the tip of the tube between two fingers, varying the pressure as the meat emerges to ensure the casing slips off at a controlled rate. The idea is to fill it thoroughly and evenly. All being well, you will end up with one very long sausage, but if the casing ruptures, perhaps due to some overzealous handle-turning, just tie a knot in it and start again.

When you run out of casings or meat, tie a knot in the back end as you did the front.

The final piece of the jigsaw is to twist the giant sausage into links (**6**). There are various pretty ways of doing this, but the simplest is to ease the meat into segments of the desired length through the casing, then twist at the gaps.

When it comes to cooking your freshly made sausages, do it slowly and thoroughly and do *not* prick the skins. If the heat isn't too high, there is little danger of the sausages bursting and you don't want them to lose their juiciness.

OTHER FRESH SAUSAGES

NICK'S CHIPOLATAS

Ideal for cocktail parties or with your Thanksgiving turkey.

Makes about 40 sausages

- 3 pounds 5 ounces finely ground pork (picnic) shoulder
- 1 pound 2 ounces finely ground pork fatback
- 1.2 ounces salt
- 0.4 ounce freshly ground black pepper
- 0.7 ounce garlic, chopped
- 0.5 ounce fresh thyme, finely chopped
- 1 ounce flat-leaf parsley, coarsely chopped
- about 4½ yards sheep casings

Make as per Paysanne Sausages on pages 14–15.

CUMIN SAUSAGES

India is a relatively sausage-free zone, but these pork-based sausages have a flavor redolent of the subcontinent.

Makes about 20 sausages

- 4½ pounds coarsely ground pork belly
- 1 ounce cumin seed, tossed in a pan over low heat for about 5 minutes until toasted
- 1 ounce black onion seeds
- 1.2 ounces salt
- 1 tablespoon plus ¼ teaspoon freshly ground black pepper
- 3¾ teaspoons ground ginger
- 1½ teaspoons ground cloves
- about 2¾ yards hog casings

Make as per Paysanne Sausages on pages 14–15.

CUMBERLAND

This is our version of the classic sausage from the Northwest of England.

Makes about 15 sausages

- 2 pounds 10 ounces coarsely ground thick pork belly
- 0.7 ounce salt
- 2¼ teaspoons freshly ground black pepper
- 1 teaspoon freshly grated nutmeg
- 1 tablespoon plus ½ teaspoon dried marjoram
- 1 tablespoon dried sage
- 2¼ yards hog casings

Make as per Paysanne Sausages on pages 14–15, forming one giant coil. Don't tie off into links.

MERGUEZ

These spicy North African sausages can be made with beef, but we prefer lamb-based ones.

Makes about 30 sausages

- 4 pounds lamb (use breast, neck, or leg, but ensure the fat content is about 25 percent), ground through a medium plate
- 1 ounce salt
- 1 tablespoon plus ¼ teaspoon freshly ground black pepper
- 0.7 ounce garlic, chopped
- 1 ounce paprika (or Spanish pimentón for a smokier taste)
- 0.7 ounce ground cumin
- ½ teaspoon ground cloves
- ½ teaspoon ground nutmeg
- about 3⅓ yards sheep casings

Make as per Paysanne Sausages on pages 14–15.

TOULOUSE

The definitive fresh sausage of Southwest France.

Makes about 20 sausages

- 4½ pounds coarsely ground pork belly
- 1 ounce relatively fine sea salt
- 1 teaspoon freshly grated nutmeg
- 2½ teaspoons freshly ground black pepper
- ⅓ cup plus 1 tablespoon and 1 teaspoon red wine
- 0.7 ounce garlic, chopped
- 0.7 ounce flat-leaf parsley, coarsely chopped
- 2 tablespoons plus 2 teaspoons chopped fresh sage
- 1 tablespoon plus 2 teaspoons chopped fresh thyme
- 2¾ yards hog casings

Make as per Paysanne Sausages on pages 14–15.

VENISON SAUSAGES

These meaty, flavor-packed sausages are perfect for grilling.

Makes about 20 sausages

- 3 pounds 5 ounces finely ground venison
- 1 pound 2 ounces finely ground pork fatback
- ½ cup plus 2 tablespoons red wine
- 1 ounce salt
- 0.4 ounce garlic, chopped
- 2½ teaspoons freshly ground black pepper
- 1 tablespoon finely chopped fresh rosemary
- 2 teaspoons crushed juniper berries
- 2¾ yards hog casings

Thoroughly mix the ingredients and fill the casing using the method shown on pages 14–15. Hang the sausages to dry for at least 24 hours in a cool, airy place before cooking.

FRESH CHORIZO

Not to be confused with cured varieties of chorizo, these sausages must be cooked before being eaten.

Makes about 20 sausages

- 4 pounds 14 ounces coarsely ground fatty pork belly
- 0.7 ounce garlic, chopped
- 1.8 ounces Pimentón de la Vera (hot, bitter-sweet, sweet, or a mixture)
- 1.4 ounces salt
- 2¾ yards hog casings

Thoroughly mix the ingredients and fill the casing using the method shown on pages 14–15. Hang the sausages to dry for at least 24 hours in a cool, airy place before cooking.

HOW TO MAKE CURED SAUSAGES

In the world of chorizo, the fundamental division is between "cooking" varieties and those designed to be eaten raw. The latter need to be cured or, in other words, rendered safe. This is done by fermentation, a preserving process that serendipitously enhances flavor. Successful fermentation involves creating the right conditions for the growth of certain benign strains of bacteria that convert sugars in the meat into lactic acid. This has two beneficial effects: it helps protect the chorizo from acid-intolerant bacteria and it gives it its lip-smacking tang.

Here we show you how to make a cured, uncooked chorizo of the kind you might be served in a good Spanish tapas bar. The authenticity of this recipe is derived from the Pimentón de la Vera. This is a high-quality paprika from Spain, available from specialist suppliers.

CHORIZO

Makes 4 to 6 chorizo

- 2¼ yards beef middles (casings)
- 4½ pounds very coarsely ground pork belly
- 0.7 ounce chopped garlic
- 0.5 ounce Pimentón de la Vera, hot
- 0.7 ounce Pimentón de la Vera, bitter-sweet
- 1 ounce Pimentón de la Vera, sweet
- ½ teaspoon (1.2g) starter culture, dissolved in 3 tablespoons warm water
- 1.8 ounces curing salt

Allow about 2 hours for making the chorizo if you're doing this for the first time. Make sure your counter is scrupulously clean, ditto your sausage-making equipment. We soak everything in sterilizing fluid for 10 minutes. Ensure your hands are thoroughly scrubbed and that there are washing facilities nearby. Gather the equipment you'll need, including a small bowl of warm water to soak the sausage casings in (to keep them moist), a sterilized pin or wooden kebab stick (to prick the casings), disposable latex gloves (to wear when handling the sausage mixture), and butcher twine (for tying off sausages). You'll also need a roll of paper towels (things can get a little messy).

Begin by soaking your beef middles in warm water until you are ready to use them. Then prepare your ingredients. We usually keep them separate so we can survey them before we pour them into the sausage mix. While you are preparing the ingredients, keep the ground meat in the refrigerator. You want it to be very cold. If it isn't, it will turn uncomfortably gluey as the fat warms up. For this reason, sausage stuffing is not a hot-weather activity.

Take the ground meat out of the refrigerator and sprinkle the other ingredients on top. Make sure you scatter them well, especially the salt. Thoroughly mix using your hands **(1)**. The meat will start off loose, but will become stickier and more compact after a few minutes.

Gently transfer the casing onto a large tube. A little water can help the process. Leave a few inches of casing hanging over the end of the tube and tie a knot in it. Fill the chamber with the chorizo mixture **(2)** and pack it down firmly. Pierce the end of the casing once or twice with your sterilized stick so that you don't get an air pocket appearing in your first sausage. You are now ready to go. Proceed as slowly as you like. If you become unsure at any stage, stop and evaluate the situation before you go any further.

Start turning the handle with one hand while the other gently guides the first sausage into being as it starts to appear from the tube.

As you start to fill the casing, bear the following in mind:
• Beef middles are very robust. Fill them thoroughly, as you want your chorizo to be nice and plump.
• Push some of the casing to the front of the tube from time to time to provide some slack. Keep it moist so it slides off easily as the sausages fill.
• Give the chorizos a little prick with your wooden stick wherever you see air bubbles appearing.
• Once you build up confidence you will be able to fill a few pounds into casings in a few minutes.

Once you have filled your casing **(3)**, tie a knot at the end of it. Then tie off the sausages into 12-inch lengths **(4)**, each with a loop at one end. Prick each sausage all over to aid the drying process **(5)**. Incubate the chorizo for 12 to 24 hours in a warm, very humid place (at around 90 percent humidity) to activate the starter culture and kick-start the fermentation process **(6)**—a hot shower left to run intermittently in a clean and sealed bathroom should do the trick.

Hang the chorizo for 6 to 8 weeks at 53.5 to 59°F at 70 to 80 percent humidity (a hygrometer and thermometer are useful here, see page 13) until their weight is reduced by approximately 30 percent. If the humidity is too low, the skins will harden, interfering with the maturing process. If it is too high, the chorizo will not dry properly and may go bad. See the picture on page 2 for the finished article!

OTHER CURED SAUSAGES

KABANOS

These Polish sausages (see pictures below and opposite) make good subjects for your early curing experiments, as they mature in just two weeks.

Makes about 30 sausages

- 0.4 ounce caraway seed
- 4½ pounds pork belly, trimmed of skin, bone, and cartilage and coarsely ground
- 0.4 ounce freshly ground black pepper
- 2½ teaspoons Colman's mustard powder
- 1 ounce curing salt
- about 3⅓ yards sheep casings

Toast the caraway seed in a pan for 3 to 4 minutes, stirring continuously. Then mix the ingredients together, place them in a shallow open tray, and refrigerate overnight.

The following day, mix the ingredients again, either in a bowl or a food mixer with a paddle attachment, until they are sticky. Then fill the mixture into the casings and tie the sausages into 6-inch links.

Dry the kabanos in a cool, airy place for 24 hours. Cold smoke them (see pages 26–27) for 6 hours, then hang them for about 2 weeks, until they are firm. Keep the temperature in the maturing room or chamber at around 53.5°F and the humidity at about 70 percent.

SALAMI

There are endless variations on the basic theme. You could, for instance, substitute about half the pork shoulder for beef, as they do in Milan, or add a splash of white wine to the basic mix.

Makes 4 to 6 salami

- 4 pounds pork (picnic) shoulder, coarsely ground
- 1 pound 9 ounces coarsely ground pork fatback
- 1.4 ounces fennel seed (optional)
- 1 ounce garlic, chopped
- 0.4 ounce cracked black pepper
- 2.5 ounces curing salt
- 2¼ yards beef middles (casings)

Make as per Chorizo on pages 18–19.

ANCHO SALAMI

Sweet and mild anchos (dried poblano chiles) give this salami a chorizo-like flavor.

Makes 4 to 6 salami

- 3 pounds 5 ounces finely diced or coarsely ground pork (picnic) shoulder
- 1 pound 2 ounces finely diced pork fatback
- 1 ounce dried ancho chiles, chopped
- 3 garlic cloves, chopped
- 2 ounces curing salt
- 1 ounce paprika
- 2¼ yards beef middles (casings)

Mix the ingredients together while they are very cold, then place them on an open tray and leave in the refrigerator for 24 hours. Fill into the casings and then let mature for 6 to 8 weeks.

MILANO SALAMI

This Italian cured sausage is one of the best-known and best-selling salamis in the world.

Makes 4 to 6 salami

- 2¼ pounds finely ground pork (picnic) shoulder
- 1 pound 2 ounces finely ground beef or veal
- 1 pound 2 ounces finely diced pork fatback
- 2½ teaspoons ground white pepper
- 3 garlic cloves, finely chopped
- 2 tablespoons plus 1 teaspoon mixed dried herbs
- ⅓ cup plus 1 tablespoon and 1 teaspoon red wine
- 1 teaspoon ground allspice
- 2 ounces curing salt
- 2¼ yards beef middles (casings)

Mix the filling ingredients thoroughly and fill into the casings. Hang to mature for 6 to 8 weeks.

HOW TO MAKE PRECOOKED SAUSAGES

A precooked sausage is one that is cooked or partially cooked as an essential part of the manufacturing process, usually by immersion in very hot but not boiling water. Some of the world's most excellent sausages fall into this category, among them Frankfurters and boudin blanc.

Many precooked sausages are emulsified. This means their contents are blended into a smooth paste in a way that ensures the particles of meat and fat become bound up with water. This makes the resulting sausages particularly moist and juicy. To achieve the requisite smoothness, the meat is typically finely ground twice.

There is no one-size-fits-all formula for making precooked sausages, but the two examples below—one emulsified, one "regular"—will give you a good grounding in the basic principles.

BOUDIN BLANC

This French delicacy shares an etymological root with the English word "pudding."

Makes about 15 sausages

- 1 pound 2 ounces lean veal breast, finely ground twice
- 1 pound 2 ounces lean pork (picnic) shoulder, finely ground twice
- 0.7 ounce salt
- 1¼ teaspoons ground white pepper
- ½ teaspoon ground cloves
- heaping 1 tablespoon porcini powder (to make this, take dried porcini mushrooms and grind them in a coffee/spice grinder until powdery)
- 1 cup plus 1 teaspoons crème fraîche or thick sour cream
- 4 eggs
- 1 ounce flat-leaf parsley
- 1¾ yards hog casings

Place the ground veal and pork in a food processor with the cutting blade inserted. Add the salt, pepper, cloves, and porcini powder and pulse about 6 times, until you have a sticky mixture.

Slowly add the crème fraîche or sour cream, eggs, and finally the parsley and blend for about 1 minute, until you have a smooth paste, attractively flecked with parsley.

Chill the mixture in the refrigerator for 20 minutes, then fill it into hog casings. Twist into sausages that are approximately 4½ inches long.

Heat up a large pot of water and simmer the boudins at between 158°F and 176°F for 20 minutes. Turn off the heat and leave the sausages in the hot water for 10 minutes more, then chill them under cold running water.

At this point you can store your boudins in the refrigerator for up to 5 days, or freeze them, but you will probably be itching to try them. They can be prepared in various ways, including any of the following:

• Heat the boudins up in water (again), then squeeze the fillings out of the casings and serve with mustard.
• Fry the sausages in a little oil with their skins on.
• Remove the casings and gently fry the contents in butter.

LUXURY VEAL SAUSAGES

These simple, flavorsome sausages go down well with almost everybody and are extremely popular with Nick's kids. The crushed ice in the recipe serves two purposes: it prevents the meat overheating due to the friction of the revolving blades in the grinder and it provides the water necessary for the formation of a succulent emulsion. Keeping your ingredients and equipment cold is always important in sausage making, but it is particularly vital when making this type of sausage. The meat you use should be at or slightly below freezing point, so give it a spell in the freezer before you start.

Makes about 30 sausages

- 1 pound 2 ounces veal breast, finely ground twice, at freezing point or slightly below
- 1 pound 2 ounces pork belly, finely ground twice, at freezing point or slightly below
- ½ pound bacon, finely ground twice, at freezing point or slightly below
- 9 ounces ice, blended into snow
- 1¼ teaspoons ground white pepper
- 0.7 ounce salt
- 2 teaspoons Colman's mustard powder
- heaping ½ teaspoon ground mace
- 3⅓ yards narrow sheep casings

In a large bowl, place the ground veal, pork belly, and bacon. Add the rest of the ingredients and stir for about 5 minutes, by which time your arm will probably be aching. Avoid this by using a food mixer with a paddle attachment. Set it to medium speed and mix until you have a smooth paste.

Fill the sausage mix into the casings and twist off at 4½ to 6-inch intervals.

Heat up a large pot of water and simmer the sausages at between 58°F and 176°F for 15 minutes. Check the temperature with a thermometer—if it rises any higher, the casings may split. Turn the heat off and leave the sausages in the hot water for another 10 minutes, then chill them under cold running water.

At this point you can store the sausages in the refrigerator for up to 5 days, or freeze them.

To cook the sausages, either fry them in a bit of oil or grill them. You could also try the recipe on page 85.

OTHER PRECOOKED SAUSAGE

FRANKFURTERS

In Germany, Frankfurters are made with pork, unlike the usual beef in the U.S. This recipe gives you both options. We like our Franks thin, hence the sheep casings, but if you like them thicker, use hog's.

Makes about 25 sausages

- 3 pounds 1 ounce pork (picnic) shoulder (ensure the fat content is about 25 percent); alternatively, use beef top round, including the surrounding fat
- 3.5 ounces smoked bacon
- 1 ounce curing salt
- 10.5 ounces ice, blended into snow
- 3½ teaspoons Colman's mustard powder
- 0.4 ounce paprika
- 1¾ teaspoons ground mace
- 2 teaspoons ground white pepper
- 0.4 ounce garlic, finely chopped
- about 2¼ yards sheep casings

Cut the pork into strips and grind it through a fine plate together with the bacon. Place in the freezer until partially frozen, then repeat the grinding process.

Mix all the ingredients together either in a large bowl or in a food mixer using the paddle attachment for about 5 minutes, until you have a smooth, sticky mass. Ensure the temperature remains close to freezing throughout.

Fill into the casings and tie off into 6 to 7-inch links.

Dry the Frankfurters in a cool, airy place for 24 hours, until the casings feel dry.

Either blanch the sausages at 167 to 185°F for 45 minutes or hot smoke them at 167 to 185°F for around 1½ hours, until their core temperature has passed 158°F. For the best of both worlds, combine the two processes by hot smoking the Franks for about 45 minutes and then blanching them.

These Frankfurters can be stored in the refrigerator for up to a week or frozen. You can reheat them in a number of ways—simmer, fry, broil, or grill.

WEISSWURST

This Munich, Germany, specialty is one of our favorite emulsified sausages.

Makes about 20 sausages

- 2 pounds 7 ounces lean veal breast or lean pork (picnic) shoulder
- 14 ounces pork fatback
- 1 ounce salt
- 14 ounces ice, blended into snow
- 1 tablespoon plus 1 teaspoon Colman's mustard powder
- 1 teaspoon ground mace
- 1.8 ounces flat-leaf parsley
- 1.4 ounces skim milk powder
- 2 teaspoons ground white pepper
- 2¾ yards hog casings

Make as per Luxury Veal Sausages on page 23, only fill the weisswurst into hog casings. These excellent sausages should be reheated in simmering water, not fried. Squeeze the contents out of the casings before serving. They can be stored in the refrigerator for up to a week or frozen.

SAVELOYS

These saveloys are a million miles from the dismal items sold in many "fish and chip" shops in Britain. Traditionally, saveloys are preserved with curing salt, which turn the meat an attractive pink color. We've used beet powder instead.

Makes about 15 sausages

- 3 pounds 5 ounces pork (picnic) shoulder, finely ground twice
- 1 ounce salt
- 2 teaspoons ground white pepper
- 1 teaspoon ground cardamom
- heaping ½ teaspoon ground mace
- 0.4 ounces paprika
- 0.4 ounces red beet powder
- 2¼ yards hog casings

Chill the ground pork until it is close to freezing. Sprinkle the salt, white pepper, cardamom, mace, paprika, and beet powder over the pork. Mix thoroughly, either with your fingers or using the paddle attachment in a food mixer, until the filling becomes smooth.

Fill into hog casings, then you can either hot smoke them at 167 to 185°F for around 1½ to 2 hours, until the core temperature of the sausages has passed 158°F (check with a temperature probe by inserting it inside a sausage). Alternatively, simmer the saveloys at 176°F for 30 minutes, cooling them under cold running water when they're done. They will keep for a week in the refrigerator, or you can freeze them.

WIEJSKA

Wiejska is one of the best-known smoked Polish sausages.

Makes about 15 sausages

- 4½ pounds pork (picnic) shoulder or pork belly, finely ground twice (aim for a fat content of around 25 percent)
- 1 ounce salt
- 1¼ ounces ground white pepper

- 2½ teaspoons finely chopped garlic
- scant 2 tablespoons dried marjoram
- 0.4 ounce sugar
- 10.5 ounces ice, blended into snow
- 2¾ yards hog casings

Mix the ingredients together either in a large bowl or in a food mixer using the paddle attachment. Ensure the temperature of the ground pork is at or slightly below freezing. Fill the mixture into the casings. Hot smoke at 167 to 185°F for 1½ to 2 hours, until the core temperature of the sausages has passed 158°F (check with a temperature probe by inserting it inside a sausage). Wiejska can be stored in the refrigerator for up to a week or frozen.

Serve either cold and sliced or fried, depending on the weather/your mood/the recipe you are following.

KNACKWURST

This short, thick, cooked German beef sausage is similar to the rindswurst we saw being made in Frankfurt (pages 90–93).

Makes about 20 sausages

- 4 pounds beef top round including surrounding fat, cut into strips and partially frozen, then finely ground twice
- 1.8 ounces salt
- 1¼ teaspoons ground mace
- 2 teaspoons ground white pepper
- 1 tablespoon ground coriander
- 10.5 ounces ice, blended into snow
- 2¾ yards hog casings

Mix the ingredients together either in a large bowl or in a food mixer using the paddle attachment. Ensure the temperature of the ground beef is at or slightly below freezing when you start. Fill the mixture into the casings.

Either blanch at 167 to 185°F for 45 minutes or hot smoke at 167 to 185°F for around 1½ hours, until the core temperature of the sausages has passed 158°F. They can be frozen or stored in the refrigerator for up to a week.

HOW TO SMOKE SAUSAGES

There are two basic methods of smoking sausages (and for that matter, foods in general): cold and hot. The crucial difference is that cold smoking adds flavor and prolongs shelf life but doesn't cook the products it is applied to, whereas hot smoking does. If a smoked sausage is designed to be eaten raw, such as Hungarian salami, it has to be cold smoked by definition. Hot-smoked sausages can be eaten without any additional cooking and some of them are designed to be, but most are heated up prior to consumption. Good examples include Frankfurters (see page 24), smoked Polish sausages or Wiejska (see page 25), and Rookwurst, a tasty Dutch sausage which we show you how to make on the opposite page.

Now to the practicalities. You have a choice between building your own smoker, which is satisfying and a lot of fun, or buying a commercial model. This needn't cost the earth. A Bradley smoker, for example, allows you to do both kinds of smoking with an excellent level of control. If you prefer to go down the do-it-yourself route, there are plenty of instructions on the internet as well as literature on the subject—you could do worse than have a look at our book *Preserved*. Essentially, you need to construct a chamber for your sausages to hang in with an opening at the

top to draw the smoke up, plus a combustion chamber to produce the smoke. This will consist of a grate, onto which you place the hardwood chips or sawdust that will smolder to provide the smoke. Never use soft woods like pine—they will taint the flavor of your sausages.

If you are cold smoking, which requires a temperature of 86°F or less, the combustion chamber needs to be some distance away from the smoking chamber so the smoke cools down en route (you'll need to link the two chambers with aluminum tubing or similar). If hot smoking, which requires a minimum temperature of around 167°F, you can place the heat source directly under the smoking chamber. Nick uses an old cider barrel as a smoking chamber, Johnny, a galvanized metal trash can. The final piece of equipment you need is a temperature probe. This will tell you a) the temperature inside the smoking chamber, which can be adjusted by changing the setting of your camping stove and/or by opening or closing the aperture at the top of the chamber, and b) the internal temperature of the sausages, which is ultimately what matters when you are hot smoking.

SMOKED ROOKWURST

There are more kinds of hot-smoked than cold-smoked sausages, so to illustrate the smoking process we've chosen rookwurst, a heavily spiced Dutch hot-smoked sausage.

Makes about 20 sausages

- 2¼ pounds veal breast, finely ground twice, at freezing point or slightly below
- 2¼ pounds thick pork belly, finely ground twice, at freezing point or slightly below
- 1 ounce salt
- 0.4 ounce freshly ground black pepper
- scant 1 tablespoon ground mace
- 2 teaspoons ground cardamom
- 1 teaspoon ground cloves
- 0.7 ounce garlic, chopped
- 10.5 ounces ice, blended into snow
- 2¾ yards hog casings

Mix the ingredients together for at least 5 minutes, until they form a sticky mass. Fill the stuffing into hog casings and tie off into links.

Hang the rookwurst in a cool, airy place for 12 hours to dry out a bit. If they are wet, they won't take up the smoke.

To make Nick's smoker, you will need a barrel **(1)**. The bottom should be open and you will need to make a small hole in the top. You will also need to screw some hooks into the underside of the lid, to hang the sausages from.

Place the barrel on some cinder blocks above a camping stove, on which you lay a metal plate. Pile wood chips such as oak or hickory on the metal plate and ignite the camping stove. You can control the heat in the smoker by varying the flame on the camping stove.

Hot smoke the rookwurst **(2, 3)** at 167 to 185°F for around 1½ hours, until the core temperature of the sausages has passed 158°F. Make sure the barrel is covered with a piece of sackcloth during this process so you don't lose the heat. You can check the internal temperature with your temperature probe by inserting it into a sausage **(4)**.

Remove the sausages from the smoker **(5)** and let dry for at least 12 hours before eating them, during which time the smoky flavors will continue to permeate through them. You can keep them in the refrigerator for up to a week.

You can eat your rookwurst sliced and cold, but we prefer them fried. They are even better if you heat them on a grill.

HOW TO MAKE BLOOD SAUSAGES

You either love blood sausages or you hate them. Don't make the mistake, though, of assuming you'll hate them just because of what's in them. They have a primal depth of flavor for which there is no substitute.

The recipe opposite is for a Spanish-style blood sausage, aka morcilla, which has a highly satisfying texture on account of the rice it contains. British blood sausages, which are generically known as black puddings, incorporate oats or barley to similar effect. French blood sausages (boudin noir) are meatier affairs, usually made without grains. In addition to blood, they typically contain offal and slow-cooked meat from a pig's head, as in the terrific version we encountered on our trip to Southwest France (see pages 52–55).

Ideally, such sausages should be made with fresh blood, but getting hold of it can be tricky. Even if you raise your own pigs, abattoirs will only save their blood for you if you provide them with suitable containers. If you manage to remember, you will have to stir the blood while it is still warm to remove the clots as they form. You may not fancy this at six o' clock on a cold morning just as you are getting over the demise of your beloved animals. The alternative is to purchase dried blood, which needs to be reconstituted by mixing it with roughly six times its weight in water. Dried blood is made up of incredibly fine particles so, unless you are happy to inhale clouds of irony powder, we'd advise you to wear a face mask of some kind. We learned this the hard way.

MORCILLA

Makes about 20 sausages

- 4 cups plus 3 tablespoons fresh pig's blood, or 5.3 ounces dried pig's blood
- 1 pound 2 ounces pork fatback, chopped into small cubes
- 2¼ pounds cooked Thai black rice or paella rice (rice swells to 2½ times its original weight, so you'll need 14 ounces of dry product)
- 3.5 ounces onion, finely chopped
- 0.4 ounces garlic, chopped
- 2 tablespoons chopped fresh thyme
- 1.8 ounces salt
- 2½ teaspoons freshly ground black pepper
- 0.4 ounces Spanish pimentón or smoked paprika
- about 4½ yards casings (either wide hog casings or beef middles; the latter will produce sausages with more interesting shapes)

Making blood sausages is a messy business, so wear latex gloves and an old apron.

If you are using dried blood, you need to combine it with about 3½ cups water to make 4 cups plus 3 tablespoons of reconstituted blood **(1)**. Do this in two stages. First, add enough water to create a smooth paste, then add the rest of the water and mix with a stick blender **(2)** so the paste is evenly diluted. If you're using fresh blood, move directly to the next stage.

Add the rice and onion to the blood **(3)** and fatback and mix together, either with a large spoon or your fingers. Then add the garlic and other seasonings and mix thoroughly **(4)**.

Fill into casings **(5)**, ensuring you tie off the ends tightly **(6)**.

Heat a large pan of water to 176°F and immerse your blood sausages in it for an hour, until fully set. Keep testing the temperature of the water with a thermometer. If it rises much above 176°F, the casings will split.

If any of the morcillas float to the surface, give them a careful prick with a needle to let the air that's causing the problem out.

When you remove the sausages from the poaching liquor, either let them cool naturally or place them under cold running water for 10 minutes to hasten the process.

FRESH SAUSAGES

What do merguez and Toulouse sausages have in common with uncured chorizo and the great British banger? The answer is they are all classified as fresh sausages, which means they haven't been cured and are sold in an uncooked state. The preservatives they contain, typically salt and herbs, are there to add flavor rather than shelf life. A couple of centuries ago, fresh sausages really did have to be eaten immediately and were therefore considered luxuries. Refrigeration and freezing have extended their life spans to around five days and a few months respectively, but they are still at their best just a few hours after emerging from the stuffing machine. The recipes in this chapter, which range from filling stews such as Toulouse Sausage and Bean Cassoulet to Toad-in-the-Hole, demonstrate the sheer versatility of fresh sausages.

KEEPING PIGS

Veal, beef, lamb, and venison all have their place in the kingdom of the meat-based sausage, but apart from areas where it is banned for religious or cultural reasons, this is a realm in which pork reigns supreme. Pig meat is so central to the sausage story that frankly we'd have felt phony writing a book on the subject if one or other of us hadn't raised a few pigs.

Keeping pigs is a big responsibility, morally as well as legally. If raising animals with the intention of killing them before they reach adulthood doesn't make you do at least some soul searching, you probably shouldn't be doing it at all. At the same time, there would be no domesticated pigs if people didn't breed them for their meat. No one is going to support pigs to the end of their natural life spans for fun—they live for up to fifteen years, breed like rabbits, and turn into thousand-pound monsters. If the pork they provide (and, therefore, a good proportion of the world's sausages) is to exist, someone, somewhere is going to have to kill some pigs.

If you eat meat and have the opportunity, there's a lot to be said for taking charge of the process by raising your own pigs. For one thing, there's a basic honesty involved. You will know in the most direct possible sense where your meat has come from, namely from endearing, sentient beasts. This will give you a reverence for the meat that is hard to feel for anonymous, store-bought packages. Secondly, keeping pigs is a lot of fun. They are endlessly fascinating and very good company. Above all though, from the perspective of this book, you will end up with fantastic pork for sausages.

With all this in mind, when Johnny moved to the country, the first thing he did was purchase a pair of Oxford Sandy and Black piglets. (Despite living in Gloucestershire, England, he comes from the adjacent county and wanted to show loyalty to the traditional pig of his native patch.) It was their successors, Boots and Albi, who provided the raw materials for many of the items featured in this book. Thanks to the generosity of his landlord, they had a nice little patch of field to destroy during their five-month residence and they never quite ran out of new territory to excavate. Pigs are compulsive rootlers and, before long, Boots and Albi had unearthed what appeared to be relics of an ancient Cotswold civilization. They also ate the charger for the electric fence when a heavy snowfall rendered it inoperative, but that's another story...

Young pigs convert their food (in this case, pig nuts supplemented by worms, slugs, grass, and several apples a day) at a prodigious rate. For every 6½ pounds Boots and Albi ate during their lives, they put on 2¼ pounds. You could almost see them growing, and because they were indulging their natural piggy behaviors, it was obvious that most of this weight gain was muscle. By the time the sad day came to load them into the trailer, they each tipped the scales at around 210 pounds. Taking them to the abattoir was inevitably painful, but it was a consolation to know that they'd enjoyed their brief lives to the full. It was even more consoling to collect several boxes of top-quality pork from the butcher two days later. The orgy of sausage making could now begin...

The pig, if I am not mistaken,
Supplies us sausage, ham, and bacon.
Let others say his heart is big
I call it foolish of the pig.

SAUTÉED SAUSAGES WITH SWEET POTATO, GOAT CHEESE & PARSLEY

SERVES 2

1 tablespoon pine nuts

4 thick fresh sausages
(e.g. boerwors)

1 tablespoon sunflower oil

2 orange-fleshed sweet potatoes,
peeled and coarsely diced

scant ½ cup crumbled goat cheese

small bunch of flat-leaf parsley,
coarsely chopped

You can make this recipe successfully with almost any kind of fresh sausage—we'd recommend Toulouse (see page 17). We've found it especially tasty when prepared with boerwors, a meaty South African specialty best cooked on the grill.

Dry-fry the pine nuts in a pan over medium heat until well toasted, about 3 minutes. Set aside.

Fry the sausages slowly in the sunflower oil until they are evenly browned, turning occasionally. This should take about 30 minutes. (Alternatively, you can grill the sausages.)

Meanwhile, boil the sweet potatoes until cooked, about 10 minutes, and then drain.

When the sausages are done, remove them from the pan or grill and cut each one into a few pieces. Set aside.

Transfer the sweet potatoes to the pan you cooked the sausages in and toss them in the remaining cooking juices over medium heat until crisped up. (If you cooked your sausages on the grill, just sauté the sweet potato in 1 tablespoon sunflower oil in a fresh pan.)

Now take a large bowl, throw all the ingredients in, including the parsley, and toss together before serving.

HAM & PARSLEY SAUSAGES WITH MELTED CHEESE & LEEKS

SERVES 4

8 ham and parsley sausages
(see below)

1 tablespoon sunflower oil

2 medium leeks, washed and sliced

1 tablespoon butter

3 medium potatoes, sliced and
boiled for 15 minutes until cooked

1¾ cups shredded cheddar

1 slice of fresh white bread, blended
into bread crumbs in a food
processor

freshly ground black pepper

The Sausages

3 pounds 5 ounces cooked ham,
freshly carved (make sure about
25 percent of it is fat)

5.3 ounces fresh white bread
crumbs, made by blending 2 or
3 slices of fresh white bread in
a food processor

2 medium onions, finely chopped

½ cup flat-leaf parsley, chopped

1 freshly grated nutmeg

2½ teaspoons freshly ground
black pepper

2¼ yards hog casings

We've never come across anyone selling these sausages, so for the recipe that follows you'll have to make them yourself. It will be worth it though. But if you're in a hurry, substitute any other mildly flavored fresh variety. You will need a medium oven dish for this simple yet rather indulgent recipe.

First make your sausages. Chill the ham and fat. Cut into strips and grind through a medium plate. Place the ground meat in a bowl, add the rest of the ingredients, and mix with your fingers until sticky. Fill the mixture into hog casings, following the instructions for making fresh sausages on pages 14–15.

When you're ready to cook, preheat the oven to 400°F.

Gently fry the sausages in the oil until they are browned all over, about 10 minutes.

While the sausages are frying, fry the leeks in the butter over medium heat for 5 minutes, stirring frequently.

Transfer the sausages, leeks, and cooked potatoes to the oven dish.

Mix the cheddar and bread crumbs in a bowl and add a sprinkling of black pepper.

Top the sausages with this mix, then bake in the oven for 20 minutes, until golden brown. Serve immediately.

SAUSAGE POT AU FEU WITH GARDEN VEG

This creamy French-inspired stew is ideal fare for late spring or early summer, when the constituent vegetables are in season. Toulouse sausages (see page 17) work well in this dish.

Gently fry the sausages in the sunflower oil, turning frequently, until golden brown, about 15 minutes.

Meanwhile, melt the butter in a large pan, then add the bacon, leek, shallot, and fennel. Replace the lid and slowly braise for 10 minutes, giving the pan an occasional shake.

Add the chicken stock and new potatoes. Simmer until the potatoes are cooked, about 20 minutes.

Coarsely slice the sausages and add them to the pan together with the peas, tarragon, tomatoes, mustard, and crème frâiche or sour cream.

Simmer for another couple of minutes and the Pot au Feu will be ready to serve.

SERVES 4

8 fresh sausages

1 tablespoon sunflower oil

1 tablespoon butter

6 thick slices of smoked bacon, chopped

1 medium leek, washed and coarsely sliced

2 shallots, sliced

1 fennel bulb, sliced

3 cups plus 2 tablespoons fresh chicken stock

16 smallish new potatoes

1½ cups petit pois or garden peas

1 to 2 fresh tarragon sprigs, chopped

10 cherry tomatoes, cut in half

2 teaspoons Dijon mustard

heaping 1 cup crème fraîche or thick sour cream

SAUSAGE WITH HOME-COOKED SPICY BEANS

4 to 8 chipolatas or Frankfurters

1 tablespoon sunflower oil

2 to 4 slices of bread, toasted

The Beans

2¾ cups dried cannellini or other white beans

½ teaspoon baking soda

The Sauce

6½ pounds fresh ripe tomatoes, chopped

1 cup plus 1 tablespoon and 1 teaspoon cider vinegar

10 cloves

4 cardamom pods

½ teaspoon ground white pepper

½ teaspoon ground mace

½ teaspoon ground allspice

¼ teaspoon ground cinnamon

2 teaspoons smoked paprika

½ cup sugar

4 garlic cloves, chopped

1 cup sun-dried tomatoes, finely chopped

The marriage of pork products and white beans is deservedly popular on both sides of the Atlantic. This recipe concentrates on the beans. As far as the accompanying sausages are concerned, high-quality chipolatas or Frankfurters come to mind, but use any broiled or fried variety you fancy. The sausage in the picture is an extra-long homemade chipolata (see recipe on page 16), coiled rather than twisted into links.

Soak the beans overnight in cold water.

To make the sauce, simmer the ingredients for a couple of hours, until they have reduced in volume by at least a quarter.

Pass the mixture through a food mill; the result will be a delicious thickened tomato sauce. The riper the tomatoes you use, the sweeter it will be.

Drain the beans, transfer to a pan, and cover with water. Add the baking soda (which helps soften the beans), bring to a boil, and simmer until soft, about 30 minutes.

While the beans are cooking, cook your chosen sausages in the oil, ensuring you time it so they are cooked just as the beans are ready (about 20 minutes).

Add the beans to the sauce. If you find there are too many of them, they freeze beautifully.

Serve on toast with the sausages.

THE GINGER PIG: U.K.

Borough Market, next to Southwark Cathedral in South East London, is a gathering place for some of the best food producers in Britain. Naturally, in a nation in which consuming them is second nature, many stalls sell fresh pork sausages. None has a better reputation than The Ginger Pig.

What makes the company almost unique is the degree of control it has over its products. The Ginger Pig breeds its own pigs, grows their feed, and converts them into superb sausages, all within the confines of a couple of farms in North Yorkshire. For Tim Wilson, the company's founder, this is just the obvious way of doing things, but in this era of commercial specialization, it is actually very unusual. The upshot is that the company exudes integrity, as do its products.

We woke up one windy March morning in a bed and breakfast randomly chosen on the internet and wondered if we were actually anywhere near Grange Farm. It turned out to be 50 yards away. On strolling into the production area, a beautiful mini stone barn equipped with huge maple butcher's blocks, we found a group of Yorkshiremen making a thoroughly unBritish product—garlic Toulouse sausages. They did, though, add bread crumbs to the mix, which would be anathema to most French butchers. Andrew, who had been given the job of showing us around, explained that they helped keep the sausages moist and gave them the texture the British public expects.

As the lads moved on to making Cumberland sausages, some more features of the company's production methods came to light. One of the most striking was the inclusion of leg meat in the mixes. Most sausage manufacturers stick to less-expensive cuts, but evidently nothing is too good for The Ginger Pig's customers. Andrew and co. do, however, add fattier shoulder meat to ensure the end products are not too dry. They aim for a fat content of around 20 percent, which they judge entirely by eye.

Another of the firm's selling points was revealed during a poke around the farmyard. They breed their pigs the old-fashioned way, without recourse to artificial insemination. To this end, a hilariously inexperienced Tamworth boar was placed in a pen with a rather more knowing Berkshire sow. Such was her exasperation that, at one stage, she clambered onto his back to show him what to do.

As this glimpse into the private lives of Tim Wilson's pigs illustrated, several rare breeds are kept on the company's farms, among them the large-rump Welsh and the stocky Saddleback.

By selective crossbreeding, he is able to ensure that the piglets have hybrid vigor and the best qualities of both parents. The one relative constant is the presence of at least some genes from the Tamworth, an elegant, long-nosed russet creature, in honor of which the company is named. Tamworths are particularly agile and mischievous and, therefore, more high-maintenance than many other breeds, but they are charming characters and their meat is superb. They are also tough, which comes in handy when it's 5°F on the moors.

SAUSAGE & PUY LENTIL STEW

This dish would be excellent made with Toulouse sausages (see page 17) but we've given it a British twist. Cumberland sausages (see page 16), traditionally sold in unbroken coils, are peppery, herby, and delicious.

Fry the sausage in the 2 teaspoons olive oil over medium heat, turning occasionally, until beautifully browned, about 10 minutes. Remove from the pan. Let cool, then chop coarsely and set aside.

Fry the carrots, onions, and mushrooms in the remaining olive oil over medium heat, turning frequently. Once browned, add the tomatoes, wine, water, bouillon cube, and the herbs. Squeeze in the soft flesh of the garlic.

Simmer for 15 minutes and then add the lentils and sausages. Gently cook for another 10 minutes, season with a small amount of salt and black pepper, and your entrée is ready.

SERVES 6

2 pounds 10 ounces sausages or large ring of Cumberland sausage

2 teaspoons olive oil, plus 1 tablespoon

4 medium carrots, peeled and sliced lengthwise

8 pearl onions, peeled

4 large mushrooms, coarsely sliced

4 tomatoes, chopped

2 cups plus heaping 1 tablespoon red wine and heaping 1 cup water

1 beef bouillon cube

4 fresh sage leaves, 2 thyme sprigs, and 1 rosemary sprig, all coarsely chopped

1 garlic bulb, top sliced off, smothered in olive oil, wrapped in foil, and baked in the oven at 400°F for 30 minutes (this can be done in advance)

2⅔ cups precooked, drained Puy lentils

salt and freshly ground black pepper

SAUSAGE HOTPOT WITH WORCESTERSHIRE SAUCE

SERVES 4

14 ounces fresh pork sausages

1 tablespoon olive oil (optional)

1 tablespoon butter

1 medium onion, coarsely diced

½ leek, washed and coarsely chopped

2 garlic cloves, chopped

2 teaspoons paprika

1 medium red bell pepper, seeded and coarsely diced

2 tablespoons tomato paste

heaping 1 cup red wine

1 to 2 thyme sprigs, chopped

2 fresh bay leaves

¼ teaspoon dried sage

3 cups plus 2 tablespoons chicken stock

3 medium potatoes, washed and coarsely diced

1 x 14.5-ounce can diced tomatoes

1 tablespoon Worcestershire sauce (we like Lea & Perrins)

Nick is a Northern English lad at heart and this recipe shows his roots. Hotpots, such as Lancashire's classic lamb and potato version, are very popular north of the Watford Gap (gateway to the English Midlands), being warming, comforting, and easy to prepare. This sausage-based example is no exception. Try a good Northern fresh pork sausage for this dish, such as a Cumberland (see page 16) or Lincolnshire sausage.

Gently grill the sausages or fry them over medium heat in the olive oil until browned, about 20 minutes. Let cool, then slice into disks.

Melt the butter in a large pan. Gently fry the onion, leek, garlic, paprika, and bell pepper for 10 minutes or so.

Add the tomato paste, wine, thyme, bay leaves, sage, chicken stock, potatoes, tomatoes, Worcestershire sauce, and sliced sausage.

Simmer until the potatoes are cooked, about 30 minutes. Serve with crusty bread and butter.

TOAD-IN-THE-HOLE

Depending on the quality of the sausages and the execution, this classic British dish can be depressingly stodgy or rather magnificent. Our "toads" of choice are pork chipolatas (see page 16) wrapped in smoked bacon, served with a flavorsome onion gravy made from rich chicken stock and a good slug of booze. For this recipe you need a standard-size 12-cup muffin pan (or, of course, two six-cup ones).

Preheat the oven to 400°F. Wrap each chipolata in one slice of bacon and bake for 15 minutes, each in an individual muffin cup.

While they are roasting, whisk the batter ingredients together in a bowl. Remove the chipolatas from the oven and immediately ladle out the batter into the muffin cups so there is a chipolata poking out of each one. Place the pan in the oven and bake until the batter is puffed up and golden brown, about 20 minutes more.

While all this has been going on, you will have been making the gravy. To do this, heat up the stock and red wine in one pan while frying the onion in the butter over medium heat in another. Continue until nice and soft, about 10 minutes. Stir in the flour and slowly pour in the hot stock, whisking as you go.

Add the thyme and Worcestershire sauce and simmer gently, stirring occasionally, then season to taste with salt and pepper.

Remove the toads-in-the-hole from the oven and serve with mashed root vegetables and ladles of gravy.

SERVES 4

The Toads

12 chipolatas

12 slices of smoked bacon

The Batter

¾ cup all-purpose flour

1 egg

1¼ cups milk

The Gravy

1¼ cups chicken or beef stock

heaping 1 cup red wine

1 medium onion, sliced

1 tablespoon butter

2 teaspoons all-purpose flour

2 thyme sprigs

2 teaspoons Worcestershire sauce

salt and freshly ground black pepper

PAYSANNE POACHED WITH SPINACH, POTATOES, MUSTARD & CRÈME FRAÎCHE

SERVES 2

4 robust fresh pork sausages

1 tablespoon olive oil

4 garlic cloves, sliced

2 red onions, coarsely chopped

3 medium potatoes,
coarsely chopped

2 cups plus heaping 1 tablespoon
chicken stock

6 fresh sage leaves, chopped

9 ounces spinach, washed and
coarsely chopped

2 teaspoons French mustard

¾ cup plus heaping 1 tablespoon
crème fraîche or thick sour cream

This creamy, flavorsome, and easy-to-cook recipe works well with any robust pork sausage such as Paysanne (see page 15), Toulouse (see page 17), or any Italian cooking sausage.

Fry the sausages in the olive oil in a large pan or nonstick wok over medium heat for 5 minutes, turning frequently. Remove from the pan and set aside. Put into the same pan the garlic and onions and fry for 5 minutes or so, stirring occasionally. Add the potatoes, chicken stock, and sage, bring to a boil, and simmer until the potatoes are soft, about 20 minutes. Add the sausages and simmer gently for another 10 minutes, then add the spinach, mustard, and crème fraîche or sour cream. Stir over medium heat until the leaves have wilted.

PAYSANNE SAUSAGE WITH PORCINI & ROOT VEGETABLES

This tasty casserole is excellent made with paysanne sausages such as the ones we showed you how to make on page 15. The recipe is highly versatile, though. You could make an equally good version with Toulouse sausages (see page 17) or any other robust fresh variety— even Fresh Chorizo (see page 17).

- - - - - - - - - - - - - - - - - - -

Preheat the oven to 350°F.

Steep the porcini in boiling water (just enough to cover them), let cool, and then chop them up. Reserve the soaking water, which you will be using in the casserole.

Place all the ingredients apart from the Gruyère in a casserole and mix them together with a wooden spoon. Don't forget the water from the porcini. Pour this in gently, as there may be a little grit at the bottom of the bowl—avoid pouring this into the casserole.

Place the lid on the dish and bake for 1½ hours.

Remove the lid and sprinkle the cheese on top. Bake for another 15 minutes, until melted and gooey.

Serve with chunky bread.

SERVES 4

heaping ⅓ cup dried porcini mushrooms

8 paysanne sausages

3½ ounces smoked pancetta, chopped

2 carrots, peeled and chopped

2 medium onions, sliced

2 medium potatoes, sliced

4 garlic cloves, coarsely chopped

6 medium mushrooms, coarsely sliced

1 x 14.5-ounce can diced tomatoes

⅓ cup plus heaping 1 tablespoon red wine

2 teaspoons Worcestershire sauce

2 thyme sprigs

2 fresh bay leaves

scant 1 cup shredded Gruyère cheese

BAKED TOULOUSE SAUSAGE WITH SAUERKRAUT & APPLES

Toulouse sausages (see page 17) couldn't be more French, but they go remarkably well with Eastern European flavorings such as paprika and caraway seed, as this recipe demonstrates. The tartness of the sauerkraut and apples cuts through the oiliness of the sausages to memorable effect.

Preheat the oven to 400°F.

Boil the potatoes in a large pan for 10 minutes, then drain off the water and add the apples. Toss the apple-and-potato mixture with the butter and honey until the butter has melted.

Transfer the apple-and-potato mix to a large oven dish along with the Toulouse sausages, sage, salt, pepper, paprika, and caraway seed. Bake for 30 to 35 minutes, until golden brown.

Remove from the oven and immediately mix in the sauerkraut.

Serve with great big hunks of buttered bread.

SERVES 3

4 medium potatoes, cut into large chunks

3 juicy red apples (try Jonagold— they don't break up in the oven), cored and thickly sliced

heaping 1 tablespoon butter

2 teaspoons honey

6 Toulouse sausages

6 fresh sage leaves, chopped

salt and freshly ground black pepper

1 teaspoon paprika

½ teaspoon caraway seed

1½ cups sauerkraut from a jar or can, squeezed to remove the liquid

BARADIEU FARM: FRANCE

The Lot-et-Garonne department of Southwest France is a region in which everything revolves around food. Delightful days can be passed doing nothing more taxing than wondering what you will have for lunch, buying it, preparing it, sleeping it off, then repeating the process with dinner. Local delights include Agen prunes, white asparagus, and, of course, sausages. To investigate the latter, we paid a visit to Baradieu Farm, home of the Chapolard family, where three brothers (Dominique, Marc, and Bruno) plus two sisters-in-law (Christiane and Cécile) were preparing their wares for the following day's market at Nérac.

The first thing we learned was the difference between saucisses and saucissons. As the splendidly moustachioed Dominique explained, the former are fresh and the latter are dried. Things evidently aren't that simple though—the first saucisses we saw had the subtitle "seches," which means dry, and they had been hanging in a stainless-steel maturing cabinet for a week! They were, however, clearly different from the adjacent saucissons. These incorporated salami-style cubes of fat and were destined to spend an additional three weeks drying in an airy barn.

We progressed to the preparation area, where the family was busily turning out saucisses de Toulouse. It was fascinating to compare the way in which the Chapolards went about their business with the boys at The Ginger Pig (see page 40), not least because the sausages they were making were ostensibly the same. The most obvious differences were the work clothes (the brothers wore hooded smocks that would not have looked out of place in the Middle Ages), the absence of bread crumbs, and the age of the animals that furnished the ingredients (the French pigs are slaughtered at twelve to fourteen months, fully twice the age of their English equivalents).

The Chapolards make their saucisses de Toulouse in two sizes: regular and chipolata. Salt and bpepper are added at the rate of ½ ounce and ⅓ teaspoon per 2¼ pounds, a formula that also applies to the delectable rustic pâté made at Baradieu. Dominique was particularly proud of the machine they used to mix the ingredients for the sausages. It had a horizontal rather than vertical screw, which, he claimed, allowed more air into the mixture and therefore produced a better flavor.

The other sausage at the center of the family's activities was boudin noir, a blood sausage that is roughly equivalent to British black pudding. Christiane explained in detail how they are made. They take a pig's head, cut it in half, and place it in a giant cauldron together with the tongue, chitterlings, some chopped bacon and skin, sliced leeks and onions, a large bouquet garni, and various internal organs (the liver is saved for pâté). The mixture is then boiled for four hours, whereupon the bones are removed and fresh pig's blood is added at a ratio of 30 percent of the total weight. Next, the solid ingredients are seasoned, ground, and stuffed into casings. The Boudins are then simmered in the original boiling liquid for another four hours at precisely 179.6°F. Finally, they are washed in boiling water, hung up to dry for a bit, and chilled.

We got our chance to sample the fruits of the Chapolards' labor later in the day, when Dominique and Christiane joined us for lunch. The saucisses seches struck the Brits present as rather an acquired taste, but the saucisson was delightful. The pièce de resistance, though, was a boudin noir, apple, and onion salad fearlessly knocked up by Nick. Monsieur was particularly taken with this dish and it made a convert of Johnny, who is a lifetime offal-phobe.

The next day we saw the Chapolards again, this time selling their sausages, pâtés, and other pig-derived goodies in Nérac's weekly market. Their stall may have been less glamorous than some of the others, but it attracted the longest line in town.

TOULOUSE SAUSAGE & BEAN CASSOULET

When we had a small chain of gourmet soup bars in London back in the late 1990s, Toulouse Sausage and Bean Cassoulet was our most popular offering bar none. Actually more of a stew than a soup, this winning combination of herby sausages, tangy sauce, and starchy lima beans is perfect on a chilly day. If you want to have a go at making the sausages yourself, see the recipe on page 17.

– – – – – – – – – – – – – – – –

Fry the sausages gently in a little olive oil until lightly browned, then let cool. Slice thickly and set aside. Reserve all the fat and juices.

Fry the carrot, celery, onion, and pancetta in the olive oil over medium heat until soft, about 10 minutes. Stir in the strained tomatoes and the stock, then add the sausage and juices, beans, bay leaf, and thyme. Simmer for 30 minutes, then season with salt and pepper to taste.

A few minutes before the end of the cooking time, preheat the broiler to its highest setting.

Sprinkle the mixture with the bread crumbs and finish off under the broiler, removing when the bread crumbs are golden brown.

SERVES 3

2¼ pounds Toulouse sausage (or other herby variety, such as paysanne)

olive oil, for frying

2 carrots, diced

2 celery stalks, diced

1 small onion, diced

1¾ ounces pancetta, diced

1 tablespoon olive oil

heaping 1 cup strained tomatoes

2 cups plus heaping 1 tablespoon chicken stock

3¼ cups cooked lima beans

2 fresh bay leaves

2 thyme sprigs

salt and freshly ground black pepper

2 tablespoons fresh bread crumbs, mixed with a little olive oil and salt

TOULOUSE SAUSAGES WITH DUCK BREAST & LIMA BEANS

SERVES 4

4 Toulouse sausages

1 pound 2 ounces cherry tomatoes, sliced in half

8 small shallots, sliced

8 small garlic cloves, chopped

1 thyme sprig and 4 fresh sage leaves, coarsely chopped

2 duck breasts, skin on, seasoned with a little salt, pepper, and herbes de Provence

2 slices of bread, cut into small dice

salt and freshly ground black pepper

1 teaspoon dried mixed herbs

2 tablespoons olive oil

heaping 1½ cups large cooked lima beans

Beans bring out the best in Toulouse sausages (see page 17) and vice versa. The two ingredients are at the heart of cassoulet, the justifiably famous stew from the Southwest of France. In this recipe, the sausages are combined with lima beans rather than haricots, with another regional specialty, duck breast, thrown into the mix. This is a wonderful recipe for communal dipping. Ideally, you should serve it in an earthenware dish.

— — — — — — — — — — — — — — — —

Preheat the oven to 400°F. Roast the Toulouse sausages in a roasting pan with the tomatoes, shallots, garlic, thyme, and sage for 30 minutes.

While the sausages are roasting, fry the duck breasts skin-side down in a skillet set over very low heat for 15 minutes, then turn them over and give them 10 minutes on the other side. They should be nice and pink. Don't worry if the breasts are done before the sausage—just leave them on the side until you are ready to use them.

Place the mini croutons in a bowl and toss them around with a small amount of salt and pepper, the mixed herbs, and half the olive oil. Transfer them to a small oven dish and roast them alongside the Toulouse sausages for the last 10 minutes of their cooking time.

Five minutes before the sausages and croutons are ready, heat up the lima beans with the remaining tablespoon of olive oil in a small pan and coarsely slice the duck breast.

Transfer the baked sausage mix, lima beans, and duck breast to a large earthenware dish, sprinkle the croutons on top, and dig in.

SAUSAGES POACHED IN RED WINE & THYME

This is essentially elegant sausage and mashed potatoes served with onion gravy. You can use any fresh sausages (see pages 14–17), but we'd recommend Italian ones with fennel seed. You'll need a large skillet.

Gently fry the sausages and onions in the olive oil until the onions have turned gooey, at least 20 minutes.

Add the red wine, thyme, tomato paste, beef bouillon cube, and sugar. Give the mixture a stir and reduce over medium heat until the volume of the wine has halved.

To make the mashed potato, peel and slice the potatoes, boil them until soft, about 20 minutes, and then drain. Add the butter, milk, cheese, and a little salt and pepper, and roughly mash with a potato masher.

Spoon out a hearty portion of mashed potatoes onto a plate and serve with the sausages and the rich onion gravy.

Savoy cabbage, boiled and tossed in butter, would be a perfect accompaniment for this dish.

SERVES 4

8 fresh sausages

2 medium red onions, coarsely sliced

1 tablespoon olive oil

½ bottle red wine

4 thyme sprigs, chopped

1 tablespoon tomato paste

1 beef bouillon cube

1 teaspoon sugar

Mashed Potatoes

6 to 8 medium potatoes

1 tablespoon butter

⅓ cup plus heaping 1 tablespoon milk

scant 1 cup shredded Gruyère cheese

salt and freshly ground black pepper

BASQUE SAUSAGE WITH OYSTERS

For maximum authenticity, you would make this luxurious appetizer with Basque chorizo, which is called *txistorra*. This can be difficult to track down, let alone pronounce. Fortunately, you can substitute any fresh chorizo (see page 17).

––––––––––––––––––––––––––––––––––––

Fry the sausages over medium heat in a skillet until nicely browned, about 10 minutes. Remove from the pan and set aside.

Pour away most of the oil from the skillet and briefly fry the zucchini in the same pan over medium heat. Remove from the heat and then stir in the parsley.

Slice the sausages on the diagonal into big chunks. Place a mound of zucchini on each plate. Top with the chorizo and position the oysters on the side. Sprinkle with sea salt and serve.

SERVES 2

2 fresh (uncured) chorizo

2 medium zucchini, coarsely grated or cut into strips

small handful of flat-leaf parsley, finely chopped

4 oysters

sea salt

MERGUEZ WITH COUSCOUS

SERVES 3

heaping 1 tablespoon sesame seeds, toasted in the oven at 350°F for 5 minutes

1 teaspoon ground sumac (a tangy spice from the Middle East)

1 teaspoon dried thyme

½ teaspoon salt

8 merguez sausages

1 cup plus 2 tablespoons dry couscous

1 tablespoon olive oil

large bunch each of flat-leaf parsley and fresh mint, coarsely chopped

juice of 1 lemon

2 tablespoons pitted green olives, coarsely chopped

2 tablespoons shelled pistachios, toasted in the oven at 350°F for 5 minutes

seeds from ½ fresh pomegranate

The merguez sausage (see page 17) is a spicy, red North African specialty, so good that the French, who are picky about these things, have adopted it as their own. Made with lamb, beef, or a mixture of both, it is traditionally served with couscous.

———————————————————

Pound the toasted sesame seeds, sumac, thyme, and salt in a mortar with a pestle. If you don't have a mortar and pestle, just mix these ingredients together in a small bowl, crushing them with a spoon as you go.

Fry the merguez in a medium skillet over medium heat, turning occasionally, until cooked, 10 to 15 minutes.

While the merguez are frying, mix the dry couscous with the olive oil and just cover with boiling water. Let soak for 5 minutes.

In a large bowl, mix the couscous with the herbs, lemon juice, olives, and any extra juices left over from frying the merguez.

Top the couscous with the pistachios, pomegranate seeds, and spice mix. Serve with the merguez and hot flatbread.

CHORIZO BAKED WITH APPLE & RED ONION

SERVES 4

4 apples, cored and cut into quarters

4 red onions, coarsely cut into quarters

1 tablespoon olive oil

16 fresh (uncured) mini chorizo, or 8 regular-size ones

heaping 1 cup hard cider

8 fresh sage leaves

2 rosemary sprigs

This is an odd-sounding yet truly delicious combination. Try making the chorizo sausages on page 17 for this dish.

Heat the oven to 350°F.

Toss the apple and onions with the olive oil in a medium baking dish. Add the chorizo, hard cider, sage, and rosemary and bake for about 40 minutes, until the liquid has become a bit gooey.

Serve with fresh sourdough bread.

CHORIZO WITH SQUID

The combination of chorizo and squid has become a staple in restaurants all over the world. Here's how to make it at home.

- - - - - - - - - - - - - - - - - - -

Preheat the oven to 475°F. Bake the bell pepper for about 15 minutes, until charred, then let cool. Peel off the skin and remove the seeds.

Place the semolina-and-flour mix in a freezer bag along with the squid and shake until the tubes and tentacles are thoroughly coated. Set aside.

Using a stick blender or small food processor, purée the bell pepper with the olive oil and balsamic vinegar until smooth. Set aside.

Fry the chorizo in a small skillet over medium heat until nicely charred on each side.

While the chorizo is frying, heat up the sunflower oil in a deep-fat fryer until it is shimmering hot and briefly fry the coated squid until crispy, 2 to 3 minutes.

Place a pile of arugula on each plate, top with the chorizo and squid, and dress with a generous swirl of the dressing.

SERVES 3

1 tablespoon semolina mixed with 1 tablespoon all-purpose flour and 1 teaspoon dried mixed herbs

8 cleaned baby squid (available frozen or on the fish counter; they usually come with the tentacles stuffed inside—these should be used as well)

3 fresh (uncured) chorizo, cut in half lengthwise

sunflower oil, for deep-frying

3½ ounces arugula

The Dressing

1 large red bell pepper

1 tablespoon olive oil

1 tablespoon balsamic vinegar

CHORIZO PAELLA WITH SEAFOOD

This dish is scented with saffron and has a rich, smoky tomato flavor. Have a go at making the fresh chorizo shown on page 17, or even the cured version shown on pages 18–19, which can also be used for this recipe. Both have a depth of flavor that really adds savor to this dish. But store-bought chorizo will be delicious here, too. Don't worry if you don't have a paella pan—use a large wok instead.

Fry the garlic, shallot or onion, and chorizo in the olive oil over medium heat for at least 5 minutes, stirring frequently.

Add the pimentón and rice. Keep the pan on the heat and "toast" the rice for a couple of minutes, stirring continuously so it doesn't stick.

Add half the stock, the saffron, and the tomatoes and cook gently until the liquid has been taken up by the rice. Add the rest of the stock and, once it has come to a boil, add the squid and shrimp.

Simmer the rice until al dente, stir in the parsley, and serve.

SERVES 4

2 garlic cloves, chopped

2 shallots or 1 medium red onion, finely chopped

2 fresh or cured chorizo (4½ to 5½ ounces), sliced

1 tablespoon olive oil

2 teaspoons pimentón (Spanish paprika)

1¼ cups paella rice

scant 3 cups chicken stock

a few saffron threads

4 tomatoes, chopped

9 ounces cleaned baby squid

9 ounces medium raw shrimp, shell-on

small bunch of flat-leaf parsley, coarsely chopped.

HUEVOS RANCHEROS WITH CHORIZO

SERVES 2

2 fresh (uncured) chorizo, sliced

½ onion, chopped

½ red chile, sliced

½ red bell pepper, seeded and chopped

7 ounces canned diced tomatoes

1 to 2 fresh oregano sprigs, chopped

salt (optional)

2 eggs

This classic Hispanic breakfast dish, which uses fresh chorizo (see page 17), will set you up for the day nicely. You will need a small to medium skillet with a lid.

Fry the sliced sausage for a few minutes over medium heat, then add the onion, chile, and bell pepper and continue to fry until the fat has been released from the chorizo, about 5 minutes or so. Give the mixture an occasional stir.

Add the tomatoes, oregano, and a little salt if you wish. Simmer for 10 minutes.

Make 2 indentations in the sauce and break in the eggs.

Place the lid on the pan and continue to cook over low to medium heat until the eggs are done to your liking, 3 to 5 minutes.

Place the pan on the table and serve yourselves.

Warm corn tortillas are an essential accompaniment.

SWEET-&-SOUR SAUSAGES

SERVES 4

8 fresh sausages or 12 chipolatas

1 teaspoon sunflower oil

1¼-inch piece of fresh ginger, peeled and thinly sliced

1 red bell pepper and 1 green bell pepper, seeded and coarsely diced

1 medium onion, coarsely diced

10 baby corn

2 teaspoons sesame seeds

small bunch of cilantro

3 tablespoons tomato ketchup

1 tablespoon sweet chili sauce

1 tablespoon teriyaki sauce

This recipe is tailor-made for Nick's Chipolatas (see page 16) and vice versa. If you want to go all-out Asian, you could use lap cheong, but ensure you steam them first. You'll need a nonstick wok for this dish.

Fry the sausages in the sunflower oil in a nonstick wok over medium heat, turning frequently, until cooked, about 15 minutes. Remove from the pan and set aside.

Using the oil that has seeped out from the sausages, stir-fry the ginger, bell peppers, onion, baby corn, and sesame seeds over medium heat until slightly charred, about 5 minutes.

Turn the heat down to low and slice in the sausage, adding all the lovely juices that flow out of them when you slice them.

Finally, add the cilantro, ketchup, and chili and teriyaki sauces and simmer for about 1 minute.

Serve with noodles or rice.

PASTA WITH WILD BOAR SAUSAGES

Wild boar sausages are strongly flavored and so go well with this intense tomato sauce. The slight bitterness of the radicchio complements them nicely, too.

Preheat the oven to 265°F. Season the cherry tomatoes with 1 tablespoon olive oil, add the rosemary and balsamic vinegar, and roast for 1½ to 2 hours, until sweet and sticky.

Broil or grill the wild boar sausages, or fry them in the sunflower oil, over medium heat until attractively charred, about 20 minutes. Slice when cooked and set aside.

While the sausages are cooking, boil the pasta and drain.

Sauté the radicchio in 2 teaspoons olive oil over medium heat for a few minutes, then place all the ingredients in a large bowl and toss them all together.

Serve topped with shavings of Parmesan.

SERVES 4

1 pound 2 ounces cherry tomatoes

olive oil

2 rosemary sprigs

1 tablespoon balsamic vinegar

8 fresh wild boar sausages

1 teaspoon sunflower oil (optional)

14 ounces dried pasta, such as conchiglie, fusilli, or penne

2 heads of radicchio, sliced

20 black olives, pitted

block of Parmesan cheese, for shaving

VENISON SAUSAGE WITH HONEY-GLAZED CARROTS

SERVES 4

8 thick venison sausages

1 teaspoon sunflower oil

1 pound 5 ounces carrots, peeled and cut into long strips

1 tablespoon butter

2 teaspoons caraway seeds

1¼ cups hard cider

1 thyme sprig

1 tablespoon honey

salt and freshly ground black pepper

Venison sausages (see page 17) usually incorporate a certain amount of pork fat, as the meat is too lean otherwise. They are robust in flavor and go very well with sweet, slow-cooked carrots.

Slowly pan-fry the sausages in the oil for 30 minutes or so, giving them an occasional turn.

Place the carrots in a large open pan along with the butter, caraway seeds, hard cider, thyme, and honey, and season with a little salt and black pepper.

Cook over low to medium heat until the cider has almost completely evaporated. There will be much stickiness at the bottom of the pan, so ensure you stir the carrots frequently—once the sauce becomes sticky, there is a tendency for them to burn.

Serve with sautéed potatoes.

PRECOOKED SAUSAGES

If a sausage is cooked, semicooked, or hot smoked (see pages 26–27) as an integral part of its manufacturing process, it falls into the precooked category. Many of the world's favorite sausages are members of this club, among them Frankfurters, boudin blanc, and saveloys. Eating a hot dog made with sausage you have created is a pleasure not to deny yourself. At the other end of the scale, this chapter includes recipes that could grace the menu of a Michelin-starred restaurant, such as the sumptuous Veal Sausage with Morels in a Creamy Sauce. Understandably, some precooked sausage makers guard their secrets jealously. A couple of the recipes in this chapter are based on varieties—saucisse de Montbéliard and Morteau—that we frankly don't know how to make. If you want to try them out you'll need to buy in the relevant sausages, either from a smart deli at home or while you're on holiday in France.

WEISSWURST WITH CREAMY SPAETZLE

SERVES 4

8 weisswurst

¾ pound dried spaetzle
(egg noodles)

1⅓ cups shredded Emmental cheese

⅓ cup plus heaping 1 tablespoon
crème fraîche or thick sour cream

2 teaspoons French or sweet
mustard

scrunched-up handful of flat-leaf
parsley, coarsely chopped (optional)

salt and ground white pepper

Weisswurst (see page 24) are delicate, creamy, white Bavarian sausages made from veal. They sneak into this chapter because they are scalded after stuffing, but don't let this fool you into thinking they have a long shelf life—Bavarians traditionally won't eat weisswurst after noon on the day they are made. The classic way of consuming them is to suck the contents out of the casing, but you probably won't mind being spared that pleasure on this occasion. If you don't have weisswurst, you can use other smooth sausages such as Frankfurters (see page 24) or Boudin Blanc (see page 22) for this recipe instead.

Prepare 2 large pans of boiling water. Remove one of them from the heat and drop in the weisswurst.

Drop the spaetzle into the other pan and boil until al dente. Drain the noodles and return them to the pan.

Stir in the Emmental, crème fraîche or sour cream, mustard, and parsley (if using), season with salt and white pepper, and dollop onto plates.

Drain the weisswurst, cut lengthwise, and peel off the skin. Place on top of the spaetzle and serve.

POTATO SALAD WITH GRILLED FRANKFURTERS

SERVES 4

3 medium potatoes

2 medium carrots

4 large eggs

8 Frankfurters

2 teaspoons vegetable oil

6 medium gherkins,
coarsely diced

2 teaspoons capers

1 flat-leaf parsley sprig,
coarsely chopped

2 scallions, coarsely chopped

1 tablespoon coarsely chopped
fresh dill

2 tablespoons good mayonnaise

1 teaspoon French mustard

2 tablespoons crème fraîche or thick
sour cream

salt and freshly ground black pepper

squeeze of lemon juice

This zingy salad is perfect for a summer party or any other time you
have a cold beer in your hand.

Peel the potatoes and cut them into ½-inch cubes. Do the same to the
carrots. Boil them together until cooked, about 10 minutes, then rinse
under cold running water to cool them down. Set aside.

Boil the eggs for 8 minutes, until hard-cooked, then peel and cut into
½-inch dice.

Cut the Frankfurters lengthwise, coat with the vegetable oil, and broil,
grill, or fry until nicely crisped up.

Place the potatoes, eggs, carrots, gherkins, capers, parsley, scallions,
dill, mayo, mustard, crème fraîche or sour cream, salt, black pepper,
and lemon juice in a larger bowl and mix together gently. Serve with
the warm Frankfurters.

FRANKFURTERS WITH PETIT POIS & MELTING CHEESE

8 Frankfurters

about 2⅓ cups dried elbow
macaroni

¾ cup plus 2 tablespoons
cream cheese

2 tablespoons heavy cream

salt and ground white pepper

2 cups frozen petit pois

small block of sharp
cheddar cheese

This comfortingly gooey dish is a proven hit with both adults and
kids. The petit pois add a touch of color to what would otherwise be
a rather monochrome dish. If you're keen to try making your own
Frankfurters to use in this recipe, follow the instructions on page 24.
Why not get the kids involved?

- -

Broil or grill the Frankfurters, then slice them into thick chunks.

Boil the macaroni in a large pan until cooked, then return to the pan
as soon as you've drained it and add the cream cheese and cream.
Stir until the cheese has melted, then season to taste with salt and
white pepper.

Add the peas and Frankfurters, then transfer the mixture to an oven
dish. Shred a generous layer of cheddar on top and broil until golden
brown, about 5 minutes.

VEAL SAUSAGE SCHNITZEL WITH MUSHROOM SAUCE

A coating of bread crumbs has as positive an effect on a good veal sausage (see Luxury Veal Sausages, page 23) as it does on a beaten out scallop of the same meat.

––––––––––––––––––––––––––––––––

Preheat the oven to 400°F.

First make the sauce. Slice the top off the garlic bulb and place the decapitated bulb on a square of foil. Season it with a little salt and pepper, drizzle with olive oil, and wrap it up into a little foil package. Bake for 30 to 35 minutes, until soft and squishy, remove from the oven, and let cool.

Fry the mushrooms in a pan with the butter until cooked, then add the sage and thyme. Take the garlic in your hand and squeeze the soft roasted paste into the pan. Cook over medium heat for another couple of minutes, stirring continuously. Add the crème fraîche or sour cream and the grated nutmeg. Stir the mixture over low heat until everything has melted together and season to taste.

Coat the sausage slices with the flour. Dip them in the beaten egg and toss in the bread crumbs until coated.

Pour enough olive oil into a skillet to pan-fry the sausage slices and cook them over medium heat for 3 minutes on either side, until golden brown. Serve with the mushroom sauce.

Sautéed potatoes make an excellent accompaniment to this dish.

SERVES 3 to 4

The Sausages

6 to 8 cooked veal sausages, coarsely sliced

2 tablespoons all-purpose flour

2 eggs, lightly beaten

4 slices of fresh white bread, blended into bread crumbs in a food processor

olive oil, for frying

The Sauce

1 garlic bulb

salt and freshly ground black pepper

olive oil, for drizzling

3 cups sliced white mushrooms

1 tablespoon unsalted butter

4 fresh sage leaves, chopped

1 heaping teaspoon chopped fresh thyme

¾ cup plus heaping 1 tablespoon crème fraîche or thick sour cream

about ½ nutmeg, freshly grated

CURRYWURST WITH FRIES

SERVES 4

8 Frankfurters

The Curry Sauce

1 medium onion, diced

2 teaspoons chopped garlic

1 tablespoon chopped fresh ginger

1 red chile, chopped

¼ cup butter

2 tablespoons curry powder

1 x 14.5-ounce can diced tomatoes

1 tablespoon tomato paste

⅓ cup plus heaping 1 tablespoon crème fraîche or thick sour cream

¾ cup plus heaping 1 tablespoon coconut cream

The French Fries

8 medium potatoes (varieties such as Russet or Yukon Gold work well), scrubbed clean but not peeled, and cut into french fries

oil, for deep-frying

flaky sea salt (optional)

If you want a recommendation for this dish, ask a German. Over 800 million portions of hot sausage with curry sauce are sold in Germany every year. You don't have to use Frankfurters (see page 24)—more or less any precooked German sausage will do.

To make the curry sauce, gently fry the onion, garlic, ginger, and chile in the butter for around 5 minutes. Add the curry powder and stir in thoroughly.

Add the tomatoes, tomato paste, crème fraîche or sour cream, and coconut cream and simmer for 10 minutes to let the spices release their flavors.

Heat the sausages in a pan of boiling water. As soon as you add the sausages to the pot, take the pan off the heat and leave it to one side until you need the sausages.

Gently deep-fry 4 servings of french fries in oil at around 230°F, until cooked but uncolored, then remove them from the oil. Heat the oil a bit more until shimmering (about 320 to 360°F) and fry the fries for 3 to 4 minutes more, until golden brown. Remove from the pan and drain on paper towels. Season with flaky sea salt, if you like.

Cut the Frankfurters into chunks, pour the curry sauce over them, and serve with the fries.

BOUDIN BLANC WITH MORELS IN A CREAMY SAUCE

This is an impressive little dish for an intimate dinner party, hence the quantities given in the recipe. Serve it as an appetizer for two, or double the quantities to make it an entrée. The morel is a reassuringly expensive dried mushroom with a unique texture and exquisite flavor. Our Boudins Blancs (see page 23) are tailor-made for this dish, but you could easily substitute the Luxury Veal Sausages (see page 22) or Weisswurst (see page 24).

Place the morels in a small bowl and just cover with boiling water. Let soak for 30 minutes, remove from the water, and set aside. Reserve the liquid—it will have absorbed delightful mushroomy flavors and you will need it later.

Gently fry the sausages in the butter very slowly for about 30 minutes, turning occasionally.

While the sausages are frying, make the sauce. First, slice the morels and lightly fry them in the butter for 5 to 8 minutes. Add the water you soaked the fungi in, taking care to omit any grit, plus the wine and chicken stock, and reduce rapidly until the sauce has become gelatinous. Throw in the parsley or chervil and crème fraîche or sour cream, simmer for 1 to 2 minutes, and the sauce is ready.

Serve the sausages with the sauce poured over, with delicate Chinese greens such as bok choy.

SERVES 2

2 boudins blancs or veal sausages

1 tablespoon unsalted butter

The Creamy Sauce

10 medium dried morels

1 tablespoon unsalted butter

¾ cup plus heaping 1 tablespoon red wine

¾ cup plus heaping 1 tablespoon chicken stock

1 tablespoon chopped flat-leaf parsley or fresh chervil

heaping 2 tablespoons crème fraîche or thick sour cream

BOUDIN BLANC WITH CRUSHED POTATOES & CARAMELIZED RED ONIONS

SERVES 4

¼ cup butter

olive oil, for pan-frying

1 pound 2 ounces red onions, sliced

1 tablespoon balsamic vinegar

2 small rosemary sprigs

4 small thyme sprigs

salt and freshly ground black pepper

20 new potatoes

5 garlic cloves, peeled

4 boudins blancs

⅓ cup plus heaping 1 tablespoon heavy cream

1 tablespoon chopped flat-leaf parsley

Whether you're eating them or making them, boudins blancs are among the least threatening of all sausages. If you want to make your own, see the instructions on page 22. If you don't, you'll find these French delicacies in specialty food stores.

Melt the butter with 3 tablespoons olive oil in a medium pan. Add the red onions, balsamic vinegar, rosemary, half the thyme sprigs, and seasoning. Simmer gently until the onions are sweet and soft, 30 to 40 minutes, stirring frequently as they cook.

Place the new potatoes in a medium pan with a tight-fitting lid along with 1 tablespoon olive oil, the garlic, the remaining thyme, and a little seasoning. Fry very gently for 30 to 40 minutes—the same amount of time that it takes to cook the onions. Give the pan a vigorous shake from time to time.

Place the boudins in a small skillet with 2 teaspoons olive oil and cook over gentle heat, turning occasionally, until golden brown.

Transfer the cooked potatoes to a bowl, add the cream and parsley, and barely crush with a fork or potato masher. Serve alongside the boudins blancs, scattered with the caramelized red onions.

BRATWURST COOKED IN BEER

4 fresh bratwurst

sunflower oil, for pan-frying

1 large onion, sliced

1 tablespoon butter

heaping 1 cup tasty beer

14 ounces collard greens, plunged into boiling water and cooked for a couple of minutes, then chilled under cold running water

⅓ cup plus heaping 1 tablespoon heavy cream

½ nutmeg, freshly grated

salt and freshly ground black pepper

The bratwurst, bound together with eggs and cream, is one of Germany's sausage aristocrats. Not surprisingly, it is thoroughly at home in a beer-based sauce.

Fry the bratwurst in a pan in a small amount of sunflower oil over low heat, turning frequently to ensure even browning, for around 15 minutes.

Add the onion, butter, and beer. Simmer until the beer has become syrupy and the onion is soft, about 20 minutes or so.

Slice the cooked collard greens and add them to the pan along with the cream, nutmeg, and seasoning.

Bring to a boil, then serve immediately with hunks of crusty bread and some butter.

BRETON SAUSAGE & WHITE WINE POTÉE

A potée is essentially a wholesome pork and vegetable soup. The Breton sausage in question is Andouille de Guémené, a large smoked sausage made from chitterlings (pig's intestines). For once we admit defeat on making this one, we buy it at our local butcher. Alternatively, you could use andouillette or virtually any other kind of sausage.

— — — — — — — — — — — — — — — —

The heart is the "plug" at the base of an artichoke, above the stem. All around it are petals (not good to eat), while deeper inside, directly connected to the top of the heart, is the fluffy choke (even less nice). To prepare an artichoke, ease your knife down the sides of the vegetable, trimming the green petals to their base where they are much paler in color. Next, plunge your fingers into the center of the artichoke and pull away the fluff and fine petals from the top of the heart. Once you have secured your prize, dice it and squeeze a bit of lemon juice over it to stop it discoloring. Set aside.

Gently fry the onion, carrot, lardons or bacon, celery, and fennel in the butter for 10 to 15 minutes in a lidded pan, giving the contents an occasional stir. Add the artichoke, potatoes, chicken stock, white wine, and herbs and simmer gently until the vegetables are cooked, at least 30 minutes.

Stir in the crème fraîche or sour cream and season lightly with salt and freshly ground black pepper.

Pan-fry the slices of andouille over medium heat until browned on each side and serve as a garnish on each portion of soup.

SERVES 4

2 fresh artichoke hearts

squeeze of lemon juice

1 onion, coarsely diced

1 carrot, peeled and coarsely diced

3½ ounces smoked lardons or diced smoked bacon

2 celery stalks, sliced

1 fennel bulb, sliced

1 tablespoon butter

2 medium potatoes, peeled and chopped

3 cups plus 2 tablespoons chicken stock

½ bottle white wine

2 fresh bay leaves, 2 thyme sprigs, and 4 fresh sage leaves

⅓ cup plus heaping 1 tablespoon crème fraîche or thick sour cream

salt and freshly ground black pepper

8 medium slices andouille de Guémené

GREF-VÖLSINGS: GERMANY

No book on sausages could do justice to the subject without a field trip to Germany. This is a country that boasts, at a conservative estimate, some 1,500 varieties and a per capita consumption of more than 65 pounds per year. The question was which part of this wurst-obsessed nation to visit. Candidates included Nuremberg, spiritual home of the bratwurst, and Munich, birthplace of the veal-based weisswurst. In the end, though, we plumped for Frankfurt, home of the most famous precooked sausage on earth.

Our first foray from our hotel spectacularly proved the point that Germans take their sausages seriously. It wasn't even technically lunchtime, but the square adjacent to the metro station was packed with sausage-eaters. The standard offering consisted of a sausage, a generous dollop of sweet, creamy *senf* (mustard), a bread roll, and a glass of beer or *apfelwein* (flat hard cider). Many of the crowd, though, had just the sausage with the mustard. The biggest surprise was the identity of the most popular variety. It was a thick beef offering known as the rindswurst. It isn't that the Frankfurters aren't fond of Frankfurters—they are—but they like a bit of variation. They also don't call them that unless they are selling them to tourists. Instead, the city's most famous foodstuff is known as the Wienerwurst.

To penetrate deeper into Frankfurt's sausage culture, we dropped into a traditional *apfelweinlokal* (hard cider bar) called Zum Gemalten Haus, which means the painted house. Sure enough, the outside of the building was decorated with a delightful apple-tree motif. We sat in the garden and ordered the house specialty. This consisted of a mound of sauerkraut decorated with four kinds of sausage: *blut und leberwurst* (blood and liver), bratwurst, two Wienerwurst, and a fat rindswurst. As tradition dictates, the dish was accompanied by a bowl of tangy green sauce made from fresh herbs. There was no danger of going home empty. Dennis, our waiter, couldn't have been more obliging. He posed for photographs and acted as though a visit from a group of sausage-loving British authors was a daily event.

The following day, we had a 7 a.m. meeting at Gref-Völsings, the city's most famous sausage manufacturer, in the Hanauer Landstrasse. It was here, in 1894, that the citizens of Frankfurt were introduced to the rindswurst. It was created to cater for the city's growing Jewish population, for whom the traditional pork-based Frankfurter was a nonstarter. Despite the earliness of the hour, the shop at street level was doing a roaring trade selling rindswurst to local workers with cups of beef broth for dunking purposes. Our main interest, however, was in what was going on in the basement, where the company makes approximately ten tons of sausages per week.

The core ingredients of Gref-Völsings rindswurst are beef neck and shoulder, which contain fat and lean meat in the desired proportions. After arriving in the production area via an ingenious rail system, the meat is placed in a giant grinder called The Wolf along with one bulb of fresh garlic per batch. After its initial grinding, the garlicky beef is transferred to a bowl cutter along with

herbs and spices. Several scoops of ground ice are added to ensure the formation of an emulsion (a suspension of fat particles in water), which is the key to the finished sausage's smooth texture. The ingredients are then cut into a fine purée with the consistency of pâté. Great care is taken to prevent their temperature rising above 46°F.

The next stage is the filling of the sausages, which at this point are surprisingly white. They are then hot smoked for 45 minutes, followed by a period in a steam cooker, which ends when their internal temperature reaches 189°F. The rindswurst are then sprayed with cold water to cool them down, before being vacuum-packaged or sold loose from the counter upstairs. Naturally, we tucked into a few before leaving the premises. They were deliciously moist, with a perfectly balanced flavor.

Gref-Völsings also make traditional Frankfurters, which are a far cry from the limp items sold from street stalls all over the planet. They are made from pork, which is rarely the case in the U.S., and have a resilience that makes biting into them a squeaky experience. They also have a noticeable tang of bacon, which is one of their defining ingredients.

HOTPOT OF ROOKWURST & KALE

SERVES 4

8 slices of smoked bacon, chopped

2 medium onions, cut into sizeable chunks

2 tablespoons butter

1⅔ cups chicken stock

2 medium carrots, peeled and sliced

2 fresh bay leaves

4 medium potatoes, sliced

4 fresh sage leaves

4 rookwurst sausages

2 apples, cored and sliced

½ nutmeg, freshly grated

14 ounces curly kale, shredded

½ glass whole milk

salt and freshly ground black pepper

Rookwurst (see page 27) is a lovely sausage from the Netherlands, laced with spices and then smoked. This satisfying hotpot can be looked on as a Dutch version of the traditional English dish of "bubble and squeak." In its native land it is known as *stamppot* or *hutspot*.

Fry the bacon and onions in 1 tablespoon of the butter for about 10 minutes over medium heat. Add the chicken stock, carrots, bay leaves, and potatoes. Gently boil until the potatoes are cooked, about 20 minutes.

Add the sage, sausage, apple, nutmeg, and kale and simmer for about 10 minutes.

Finally, add the milk and remaining tablespoon of butter and give everything a good stir. You may even want to use a potato masher to make the mixture appealingly mushy.

Season with salt and black pepper and serve. If you have Dutch guests, they may have tears in their eyes.

SAVELOY & VEGETABLE TEMPURA

SERVES 4 AS AN
APPETIZER

¾ cup plus heaping 1 tablespoon
all-purpose flour

¾ cup plus heaping 1 tablespoon
water

⅓ cup plus heaping 1 tablespoon
milk

oil, for deep-frying

8 fresh sage leaves

2 zucchini, sliced

8 baby corn, sliced in half lengthwise

16 sugar snap peas

2 to 3 large saveloys, sliced

The Dressing

½ cup mayonnaise

juice of 1 lemon

1 garlic clove, finely chopped

dash of salt and a little freshly
ground black pepper

20 chives, chopped

Saveloys (see pages 24–25) are familiar to the British as alarmingly red sausages sold in "fish and chip" shops. Often deep-fried in batter, they don't have the most glamorous reputation, not least because it can be anyone's guess what's in them. Yet the saveloy has a noble history (it is ultimately descended from a Roman pig's brain sausage called the Cerebrus) and we think it deserves rehabilitation. Here it is given a contemporary Japanese treatment.

Begin by making the dressing. Place the mayonnaise in a bowl, then add the lemon juice, garlic, salt, black pepper, and chives and whisk together. Set aside.

To make the tempura batter, in a medium bowl, mix the flour, water, and milk together.

Heat the oil in a deep pan, preferably a wok, to 350°F.

Briefly dip the sage leaves in the batter and immediately transfer them to the oil. Deep-fry until golden brown, about 2 minutes, then place on paper towels to soak up the excess oil.

Repeat this process with the rest of the ingredients in small batches.

Serve the tempura with the dressing on the side.

SWISS CHARD BAKED WITH FRANKFURTERS & GRUYÈRE

There's no point pretending this is a dish designed with the dieter in mind, but it certainly hits the spot. You could always burn off a few calories by making the sausages yourself—the recipe is on page 24.

— — — — — — — — — — — — — — — —

Preheat the oven to 400°F.

Wash the Swiss chard and blanch it in boiling water for a couple of minutes. Drain, chill under a cold running water, and then cut into manageable pieces.

Mix the butter and mustard with the warm potatoes, then transfer to a medium oven dish with the Frankfurters, chard, crème fraîche or sour cream, and 1 cup of the Gruyère.

Season with salt and pepper, mix together loosely, and top with the remaining Gruyère.

Bake in the oven for 30 minutes, until crisped, then serve immediately.

bunch of Swiss chard, weighing around 1 pound 2 ounces

1 tablespoon butter

2 teaspoons French mustard

6 medium potatoes, sliced and boiled for around 20 minutes until soft

10 Frankfurters or other cooked emulsified sausages such as bratwurst

heaping 1 cup crème fraîche or thick sour cream

1⅓ cups shredded Gruyère cheese

salt and freshly ground black pepper

SMOKED SAUSAGE CHOUCROUTE

This version of choucroute is made with fresh cabbage as opposed to sauerkraut. An Alsacien might not consider this dish entirely authentic, but it is easy to make and quite delicious. Use smoked sausages for this recipe—such as Frankfurters (see page 24) or Knackwurst (see page 25)—combined with a coarsely ground country sausage such as Toulouse (see page 17).

Dry-fry the mustard and caraway seeds in a small pan over medium heat until the mustard seeds start to pop. Pour the seeds into a small bowl and set aside.

You will need to use a large pot that has a lid for this recipe. Fry the pancetta or bacon and onion in the butter quite gently until the onion is soft, about 20 minutes, then add the mustard and caraway seeds, bay leaves, cloves, and juniper berries. Pour in the white wine and vinegar, add the potatoes, and simmer for 20 minutes.

Add the cabbage and sausage and cook slowly with the lid on for 10 minutes.

Add the crème fraîche or sour cream and chopped parsley, season with salt and white pepper, and simmer for a few minutes more.

Serve the choucroute with mustard, beer, and rye bread.

SERVES 4

2 teaspoons black mustard seeds

2 teaspoons caraway seeds

1 pound 2 ounces smoked pancetta or smoked bacon, cut into bite-size pieces

2 red onions, thinly sliced

1 tablespoon butter

3 fresh bay leaves

6 cloves

6 juniper berries

½ bottle white wine

3 tablespoons plus 1 teaspoon white wine vinegar

2 medium potatoes, peeled and sliced

1 small head of savoy or other cabbage, cored and very thinly sliced

4 smoked sausages, thickly sliced

4 coarsely ground country sausages

1 tablespoon crème fraîche or thick sour cream

2 tablespoons parsley, freshly chopped

salt and ground white pepper

WIEJSKA WITH ROASTED GARLIC MASH

1 garlic bulb

olive oil, for drizzling and pan-frying

2 rosemary sprigs

4 medium to large potatoes, peeled and coarsely chopped

2 red onions, sliced

4 slices of smoked bacon, sliced

3½ cups baby spinach leaves or coarsely chopped larger spinach leaves

1 tablespoon butter

1 teaspoon English or Polish mustard

2 teaspoons crème fraîche or thick sour cream

salt and ground white pepper

12 thick slices of wiejska sausage

Wiejska are popular Polish sausages that are slightly smoked and flavored with marjoram. You can eat them raw, but they are delicious lightly sautéed or grilled. If wiejska prove elusive, make them yourself using the recipe on page 25, or try making this dish with any precooked sausages that appeal to you.

‒ ‒ ‒ ‒ ‒ ‒ ‒ ‒ ‒ ‒ ‒ ‒ ‒ ‒ ‒ ‒ ‒

Preheat the oven to 400°F.

Chop the top off the garlic bulb and scrunch it up in a piece of foil with a good drizzling of olive oil and a rosemary sprig. Roast in the oven for 35 to 40 minutes, until soft.

Boil the potatoes until soft, about 20 minutes, then drain and set aside.

While the potatoes are cooking, slowly fry the onions, bacon, and the other rosemary sprig in 1 tablespoon olive oil.

Stir the spinach into the onions and then add the butter, boiled potatoes, mustard, and crème fraîche or sour cream. Squeeze in the pulp from the roasted garlic and apply a potato masher. Season to taste.

Briefly fry the wiejska in 2 teaspoons olive oil and serve with the mash.

KNACKWURST WITH FIVE-SPICE

Germany meets China in this surprising but excellent concoction.
Like many emulsified sausages, Knackwurst (see page 25) are usually
poached prior to consumption, but not often in a spicy Asian stock.

━ ━ ━ ━ ━ ━ ━ ━ ━ ━ ━ ━ ━ ━ ━ ━ ━ ━

Simmer the chicken stock with the star anise, ginger, teriyaki sauce,
and knackwurst for 10 minutes.

As the stock simmers, stir-fry the long-stem broccoli and bell pepper
for a couple of minutes over high heat, stirring continuously. Transfer
to the spiced stock, then stir in the noodles and serve immediately.

SERVES 2

2 cups plus heaping 1 tablespoon
chicken stock

4 whole star anise

1 tablespoon shredded fresh ginger

1 tablespoon teriyaki sauce

4 knackwurst

6 florets long-stem broccoli or other
green vegetable

1 red bell pepper, seeded and cut
into strips

1½ cups cooked rice noodles

KIELBASA KRAKOWSKA WITH RED CABBAGE & CARAWAY

The smoked sausage in this recipe, flavored with allspice, coriander, and garlic, hails from Krakow, the city of pickles. If you can't find it, you can substitute kielbasa. The red cabbage gives this dish a suitably Central European character.

— — — — — — — — — — — — — — — — —

Gently cook the cabbage, port, apples, caraway seeds, and vinegar in a lidded pan for 30 minutes, stirring occasionally.

Slice the Krakowska and fry in the sunflower oil for 1 minute on each side. Stir into the cabbage, sprinkle with the dill, and serve.

1 small red cabbage

heaping 1 cup port

2 rosy apples, sliced

2 teaspoons caraway seeds

2 tablespoons balsamic vinegar

9 ounces Krakowska, peeled and thinly sliced

2 teaspoons sunflower oil

scattering of chopped fresh dill

KIELBASA WITH PIEROGI

SERVES 4

2 tablespoons sunflower oil

1 onion, finely chopped

9 ounces kielbasa or precooked sausages of your choice, sliced

1 flat-leaf parsley sprig, chopped

The Pierogi Dough

1½ cups plus 1 tablespoon all-purpose flour, plus extra for dusting

½ teaspoon salt

1 large egg

½ cup plus 1 tablespoon sour cream

¼ cup butter

The Filling

scant 1 cup shredded Gruyère cheese

1 large potato, peeled, cubed, and boiled until soft

salt and ground white pepper

small bunch of flat-leaf parsley, chopped

Kielbasa is the generic name for Polish sausages, most of which are smoked. One of the best ways to enjoy them is to broil, grill, or pan-fry them, or simmer them in water, then serve with fried pierogi, Eastern European dumplings reminiscent of ravioli. Pierogi are semicircular and can be stuffed with a variety of fillings. The Gruyère and potato filling in this instance is satisfying in the way that only a full-on carbohydrate hit can be.

To make the filling, mix the Gruyère with the potato, salt, pepper, and parsley in a small bowl until mushy.

To make the pierogi dough, mix the flour and salt together in a large bowl. Add the egg, sour cream, and butter and stir in thoroughly. Turn out onto a counter lightly dusted in flour and knead for a few minutes or, alternatively, pulse in the food processor until smooth (8 good pulses should do it). Roll out thinly and cut into 2½–3¼-inch circles— you should have at least 12 circles.

Fill one half of each dough circle with the cheese mix, fold over the other half of the dough, squeeze out any air, and press down the edges to seal.

Heat up a pot of boiling water and simmer the dumplings for 5 minutes. Remove from water when cooked and set aside.

Heat the oil in a large skillet. Fry the onion and sausage over medium heat for 5 minutes. Remove from the pan with a slotted spoon, leaving the oil behind, and use this to fry the pierogi on each side until they are lightly browned.

Serve the pierogi mixed with the sausage and onion and a generous scattering of chopped flat-leaf parsley.

VIENNA MACARONI & CHEESE

Confusingly, in Frankfurt, Frankfurters (see page 24) are known as Wieners, while in Vienna (Wien), Wieners are known as Frankfurters. Why each city should want to blame the other for the existence of these world-famous sausages is a mystery. Whatever you choose to call them, they definitely enhance a macaroni and cheese.

Boil the cauliflower for 3 to 4 minutes in a large pot. Immediately cool under cold running water, leaving the hot cooking water in the pan.

Cook the macaroni in the cauliflower water until al dente, then drain it and return it to the pan. Add the cream cheese, Frankfurters, cauliflower, crème fraîche or sour cream, salt, and white pepper and stir over very low heat until the cream cheese has melted. This should take about 1 minute.

Preheat the broiler to its highest setting.

Transfer the contents of the pan to an oven dish. Shred a generous layer of cheddar cheese on top, then brown under the broiler and serve.

SERVES 4

1 cauliflower, cut into bite-size florets

2¾ cups dried elbow macaroni

¾ cup plus 2 tablespoons cream cheese

6 Frankfurters, sliced

⅓ cup plus heaping 1 tablespoon crème fraîche or thick sour cream

salt and ground white pepper

sharp cheddar cheese, for shredding

SAUCISSE DE MONTBÉLIARD WITH FENNEL & MELTED CHEESE

Montbéliard is one of a number of French towns near the Swiss border with a reputation for fine smoked pork sausages. You could use other robust cooking sausages for this dish, but they need to be smoked to give it the requisite sweet-smoky flavor.

Preheat the oven to 350°F.

Mix the olive oil, white wine, fennel, and Montbéliard sausages together in an oven dish, then cover with a lid or foil and bake for 1 hour.

Remove the dish from the oven and increase the heat to 400°F.

Stir in the crème fraîche or sour cream and mustard, then coarsely slice the Camembert and lay it in slices on top of the fennel and sausages. Replace the dish in the oven and bake for 10 minutes.

Serve with crusty bread.

SERVES 2

1 tablespoon olive oil

2 cups plus heaping 1 tablespoon white wine (preferably sweet)

2 medium fennel bulbs, sliced lengthwise

2 Montbéliard sausages or other smoked sausages, cut in half

2 tablespoons crème fraîche or thick sour cream

2 teaspoons Dijon mustard

5½ ounces Camembert or other similar soft cheese

STUFFED HOTDOGS

SERVES 2

1 medium onion, sliced

1 tablespoon sunflower oil

3 medium potatoes, peeled and diced

1 tablespoon butter

2 tablespoons milk

salt and freshly ground black pepper

4 medium Frankfurters

2 tablespoons shredded Gruyère, Emmental, or cheddar

½ teaspoon paprika

Would you like to perk up your Frankfurters or add a little something to your Wieners? This recipe provides a satisfying variation on the hotdog theme and goes down very well with children, who may prefer the milder taste of Emmental or cheddar in the cheese topping.

Heat the broiler to its maximum setting.

Gently fry the onion in the sunflower oil until soft, about 10 minutes.

Meanwhile, boil the potatoes until soft, about 10 minutes. Drain and then mash them with the butter, milk, salt, and pepper.

Cut the Frankfurters lengthwise so that they are splayed out. Place them, cut-side up, on a cookie sheet that will fit comfortably under the broiler.

Spread the mashed potato on the Frankfurters and top with the fried onions.

Finally, scatter over the cheese and sprinkle over the paprika.

Broil for 10 minutes, transfer to plates, and serve with mild mustard.

ROASTED VEGETABLES WITH GARLIC & SMOKED SAUSAGE

A fabulous recipe with any precooked smoked sausage such as Wiejska (see page 25), Kabanos, or Frankfurters (see page 24). Not for the garlic-timid, this dish is best served warm with brown rice.

Heat the oven to 400°F.

Place the butternut squash, eggplant, bell pepper, mushrooms, zucchini, tomatoes, sage leaves, garlic, and thyme in a large oven dish or a roasting pan. Drizzle with the olive oil and give the dish a little shuffle. Make sure the ingredients aren't sitting on top of each other. If they are, you need a bigger dish.

Bake for 40 minutes, until the butternut squash is soft and the vegetables look enticingly caramelized.

Immediately stir in the sausages and the mascarpone. Season with a small amount of salt and pepper.

SERVES 4

1 small butternut squash, peeled, seeded, and coarsely chopped

1 small eggplant, coarsely chopped

1 red bell pepper, seeded and coarsely chopped

8 medium mushrooms

2 zucchini, coarsely sliced

4 large tomatoes

8 fresh sage leaves

1 garlic bulb, separated into cloves and peeled

2 thyme sprigs

5 tablespoons olive oil

9 ounces smoked sausage, sliced

heaping 1 cup mascarpone

salt and freshly ground black pepper

CURED SAUSAGES

The distinctive tangy flavors of cured sausages are the result of fermentation, which is a process that must be managed with the greatest care. Properly prepared salamis and chorizos are like living organisms. In fact, they are teeming with them, in the form of benign bacteria. Tending to maturing fermented sausages is like looking after hypersensitive babies. You'll find yourself running around doing absurd things to get the temperature and humidity right for these little guys, like running hot showers in the middle of the night and stuffing the extractor fan with tissues. But the effort will be worth it. Your pride and delight when you taste your first carefully nurtured salami will be beyond words. Cured sausages are particularly at home in Mediterranean-style dishes and most of the recipes in this chapter have a whiff of southern Europe about them.

SALAMI IN BRIOCHE WITH GRUYÈRE

When told the Parisians were facing an acute bread shortage, Marie Antoinette supposedly quipped "let them eat cake." What she actually said was "let them eat brioche." It still wasn't the most tactful comment, but brioche is a lot closer to bread than the mistranslation implies. Here it is used to make a savory treat that lies somewhere between glorified French toast and an upscale toasted sandwich. Salami, of course, is easy to get hold of, but if you'd like to try making your own, the recipe is on page 20.

— — — — — — — — — — — — — — — — — — — —

Take a slice of brioche and arrange 3 slices of salami on top. Then take half the cheese and sprinkle it over the salami, followed by another slice of brioche. Now repeat the procedure with the remaining ingredients.

Lightly beat the eggs and milk together and dip the sandwiches in the mixture, turning them over to ensure they are thoroughly coated.

Gently heat a skillet and pour in enough olive oil to lightly coat the surface. Slowly "fry-toast" the sandwiches for 7 to 10 minutes on each side, until the cheese inside has melted.

MAKES 2 SANDWICHES

4 slices of brioche

6 slices of salami

heaping ½ cup shredded Gruyère cheese

2 eggs

2 tablespoons milk

olive oil, for pan-frying

SALCHICHON SALAD WITH BAKED CHERRY TOMATOES

The Salad

20 cherry tomatoes

olive oil, for drizzling

2 teaspoons balsamic vinegar

salt and freshly ground black pepper

a few crunchy lettuce leaves, coarsely torn

1¾ ounces salchichon, sliced as thinly as you can

1 avocado, pitted, skinned, cut into quarters, and tossed in the juice of ½ lemon

¼ cucumber, sliced

20 fresh mint leaves

The Dressing

¼ cup olive oil

1 tablespoon balsamic vinegar

2 teaspoons Dijon mustard

1 teaspoon honey

juice of ½ lemon

salt and freshly ground black pepper

The simplicity of this salad allows the quality of the salchichon to shine through. This recipe also works well with our Salami (see page 20).

Preheat the oven to 300°F.

Arrange the tomatoes in an oven dish. Cover with a drizzling of olive oil, the balsamic vinegar, and a little salt and pepper, and bake them for an hour, until shriveled.

Place the ingredients for the dressing in a plastic container with a tight-fitting lid and give it a good shake.

Place the lettuce leaves in a shallow bowl and top with the cherry tomatoes, salchichon slices, avocado quarters, cucumber and mint.

Dress the salad liberally and serve.

SLOW-COOKED PORK BELLY WITH RED WINE & CURED SAUSAGE

The British are slowly coming around to the merits of pork belly, having previously used it just for making bacon. This meltingly tender casserole should be slow cooked. Within reason (i.e. up to about eight hours), the longer you cook it, the better it will be. You will need a large oven dish for this recipe.

Preheat the oven to 265°F.

Remove the skin from the pork belly by turning it upside down so that the skin is touching the cutting board and running a knife away from you carefully to part it from the meat.

Place the salami, Chianti, shallots, garlic, fennel, tomatoes, and bay leaves in the oven dish and lay the pork belly on top.

Drizzle with a little olive oil and season with salt and pepper. Don't overdo the salt, as the salami will release its own.

Cover the oven dish with a lid or foil and cook for at least 4 and as many as 8 hours.

Remove the lid and increase the heat to 350°F. Continue cooking for 30 minutes to concentrate the flavors.

Serve with fresh seasonal vegetables and mashed potatoes.

SERVES 4

thick chunk of pork belly, weighing around 5½ pounds

5½ ounces fennel salami, thinly sliced and cut into strips

½ bottle Chianti

8 small shallots, peeled

6 garlic cloves, peeled

2 fennel bulbs, coarsely sliced

6 tomatoes, sliced

2 fresh bay leaves

olive oil, for drizzling

salt and freshly ground black pepper

ARTICHOKE SALAD WITH SALAMI, WALNUTS & PARMESAN

SERVES 2

The Salad

6 baby artichokes

squeeze of lemon juice

olive oil, for frying

16 thin slices of salami

12 cherry tomatoes, cut in half

The Walnut Pesto

about 3½ ounces arugula

30 walnut halves, toasted in the oven at 350°F for 5 to 8 minutes until slightly browned

2 tablespoons olive oil

juice of 1 lemon

1 tablespoon grated Parmesan cheese

This crunchy, texturally rich salad is perfect for al fresco dining.

Pull the outer leaves off the artichokes and trim the stems. Cut in half lengthwise and pull out the chokes (the fluffy bits in the middle). Cut the artichoke heart into quarters and reserve in a small bowl of water, adding a squeeze of lemon juice to prevent discoloration.

To make the pesto, blend or chop half the arugula and half the walnuts together until you have a mixture with a nicely granulated texture. Add the olive oil, lemon juice, and Parmesan and mix thoroughly.

Pour olive oil into a skillet—it needs to be ¾–1¼ inches deep. Heat the oil to around 350°F. If a wooden implement sizzles slightly when dipped in the oil, it's hot enough. Dry the artichokes on a paper towels, then fry them for 8 to 10 minutes, turning once, until crispy.

Combine the artichokes, salami, tomatoes, and remaining arugula and walnuts in a large bowl and dress with the walnut pesto.

ITALIAN SAUSAGE WITH TOMATO & SAGE SAUCE

SERVES 2

2 garlic cloves, chopped

2 shallots, sliced

3½ ounces salami, thinly sliced

2 tablespoons olive oil

heaping 1 cup red wine

1 x 14.5-ounce can diced tomatoes

½ teaspoon fennel seed

6 fresh sage leaves, chopped

7–9 ounces dried pasta of your choice

12 fresh sage leaves, used whole

oil, for deep-frying

⅓ cup plus heaping 1 tablespoon crème fraîche or thick sour cream

grated Parmesan cheese, to serve

This is an excellent recipe for using up any salami you may have hanging around in the deeper recesses of your refrigerator. Serve it with your favorite pasta and plenty of Parmesan.

Gently fry the garlic, shallots, and sliced salami in the olive oil until soft, about 8 to 10 minutes.

Add the red wine, tomatoes, fennel seed, and chopped sage leaves. Simmer for 20 minutes, stirring frequently.

While the sauce is simmering, cook the pasta and deep-fry the whole sage leaves. The oil in which you do this needs to be at around 340°F—in other words, shimmering. Fry the sage leaves until crispy, about 1 minute, then drain on paper towels.

Finally, spoon the crème fraîche or sour cream into the sauce and stir in thoroughly. Serve the pasta mixed with the sauce and topped with grated Parmesan and the crispy sage leaves.

BORLOTTI BEANS WITH FENNEL & SALAMI

This is the kind of simple yet satisfying dish you might expect to be served in a farmhouse kitchen in Tuscany. Fennel and salami somehow seem to be made for each other.

Preheat the oven to 350°F.

Place the fennel, garlic, salami, cherry tomatoes, and white wine in an oven dish. Spoon over the olive oil and bake for about 1 hour, until cooked.

While the above mixture is baking, cook the borlotti beans. Place them in a large pan, cover them with water, and add the baking soda. Bring to a boil and cook, simmering, until soft, about 20 minutes.

Mix the beans into the fennel mixture, adding salt, pepper, and the parsley.

Sprinkle with the garlic-infused bread crumbs and an additional grind of salt and pepper, then bake until golden brown, about 20 minutes more.

SERVES 4

3 fennel bulbs, coarsely sliced

4 garlic cloves, sliced

7 ounces salami, sliced and cut into half moons

20 cherry tomatoes, cut in half

heaping 1 cup dry white wine

2 tablespoons olive oil

1¼ cups dried borlotti beans, soaked in cold water overnight

½ teaspoon baking soda

salt and freshly ground black pepper

small bunch of flat-leaf parsley, chopped

2 slices of white bread, blended into bread crumbs in a food processor with 2 garlic cloves

SALAMI & OLIVE OIL FOUGASSE

Fougasse is essentially a visually striking French flatbread with holes in it. It is easy to make and becomes deliciously charred around the edges of the holes as it bakes. This version is given a savory boost by the addition of chopped salami.

You'll be making 2 batches of dough for this recipe, a day apart, so ensure you have enough ingredients for both batches before you start.

Place the flour, yeast, and salt in a food processor. Using the dough-making blade, pulse once or twice, then continue to do so as you add the olive oil and water through the feed tube. The dough will form into a ball. Place it in a bowl and leave it in the refrigerator overnight covered with plastic wrap.

The following day, make another batch of dough in the same way and loosely fold it into the day-old dough together with the chopped salami. Place the enriched dough in a bowl covered with a damp dish towel and leave it to rise for a couple of hours in a warm place.

Preheat the oven to its maximum setting.

Turn out the dough onto your counter and sprinkle a little flour on it. Cut the dough into 4 equal pieces and shape each into a ball.

Sprinkle a baking sheet with flour, or semolina if you have it. You'll have to bake the fougasse one at a time, as they probably won't fit on the same sheet.

Press out one ball of dough into a triangle. Cut a slit down the center of the triangle without going all the way to the apex or base, then gently pull the sides apart until a leaf shape opens up in the middle of the triangle. Cut 2 more slits into the dough on each side of the "leaf" and pull apart as before. You should have 5 leaf-shaped holes. Place on the baking sheet and bake the fougasse for 10 minutes, until golden brown.

Repeat the process with the other 3 balls of dough.

MAKES 4

semolina, for dusting (optional)

For Each Batch of Dough (you will therefore need twice the quantities specified below)

4½ cups white bread flour, plus extra for dusting

3¼ teaspoons fresh yeast

1½ teaspoons salt

3 tablespoons olive oil

1¼ cups water

3½ ounces salami, chopped

SALAMI & EGGPLANT BAKE

SERVES 4

2 medium eggplants

olive oil, for drizzling

6 large tomatoes

2 balls mozzarella, weighing
about 4½ ounces each

5½ ounces salami, thinly sliced

dried mixed herbs, to taste

sea salt and freshly ground
black pepper

small block of Parmesan cheese,
for grating

This gooey Italian casserole combines salami with eggplant, a very tasty
pairing, and is a great dish for summer, when tomatoes and eggplants
are at their best. You will need a medium roasting pan.

Preheat the oven to 400°F.

Slice each eggplant into 6 to 8 slices. Lay them in a single layer in a
roasting pan and drizzle with olive oil. Bake for 10 minutes. In the
meantime, slice the tomatoes and mozzarella.

Starting at one end of the roasting pan, lay the eggplant, tomato,
mozzarella, and salami slices against each other at an angle so they
overlap, forming what look like slightly collapsed rows of books.

When the dish is full, season with mixed herbs, some freshly ground
black pepper, and a small amount of sea salt, and sprinkle with some
grated Parmesan. Finish off with a drizzling of olive oil.

Bake for around 35 minutes, until the protruding ingredients are
crispy. Serve with warm garlic bread.

MINESTRONE WITH FENNEL SALAMI

The Italians frequently add fennel seed to their salami mixes (see page 20), knowing from long experience how well the flavors combine. This hearty, flavor-packed soup is a good way to prove it to yourself. Even if you use regular salami, you'll still get a fennel hit from the bulb.

Pour about 1 tablespoon olive oil into a large pan and gently fry the salami, shallots, garlic, fennel, and bell pepper until soft, about 1 minute.

Add the tomatoes, tomato paste, stock, rosemary, and bay leaves. Simmer for 15 minutes. Add the beans and oregano.

While the soup is cooking, fry the croutons in the remaining tablespoon olive oil over medium heat. Keep stirring and they should be nicely toasted in about 5 minutes.

Serve the minestrone with the croutons on top.

SERVES 4

about 2 tablespoons olive oil

5½ ounces fennel salami or other salami, coarsely chopped

2 medium shallots, coarsely chopped

2 garlic cloves, chopped

1 fennel bulb, coarsely chopped

1 red bell pepper, seeded and coarsely chopped

1 x 14.5-ounce can diced tomatoes

1 tablespoon tomato paste

2 cups plus 1 heaping tablespoon vegetable or chicken stock

1 rosemary sprig

2 fresh bay leaves

1 x 14-ounce can small white beans, drained

1 tablespoon chopped fresh oregano

2 slices of bread, cut into small squares and seasoned with dried mixed herbs, salt, and freshly ground black pepper

TOMATOES STUFFED WITH GREEN OLIVES, SALAMI & PARMESAN

SERVES 4

6 large tomatoes

18 green olives, pitted

9-ounce chunk of salami, diced into small pieces

6 medium white mushrooms, diced

2 teaspoons capers

1 tablespoon chopped flat-leaf parsley

1 teaspoon chopped fresh thyme

2 garlic cloves, chopped

1 tablespoon olive oil

2 tablespoons freshly grated Parmesan cheese

freshly ground black pepper

pine nuts, for sprinkling

We would advise you to choose your tomatoes for this dish well. If you use flavorless ones, as are all too common in Northern climates off-season, it won't be quite the same, so make sure the tomatoes you use are plump and ripe.

Preheat the oven to 350°F.

Cut the tomatoes in half and scoop out the insides with a spoon. Place on a nonstick baking sheet.

In a large bowl, mix the olives, salami, diced mushrooms, capers, parsley, thyme, garlic, olive oil, and Parmesan together and season with black pepper.

Spoon the mixture into the hollowed-out tomato halves and sprinkle pine nuts on top.

Bake for 35 to 40 minutes, until the topping is attractively browned.

Serve with steamed rice.

CHORIZO & SPINACH SOUP

Chorizo (see pages 18–19) goes well with many things and spinach is certainly one of them. Making this tasty dish is an excellent way of using up a length of dried sausage lounging around aimlessly at the back of the refrigerator.

Gently fry the chorizo, celery, garlic, and onion in the olive oil in a pan for 10 minutes or so. Add the pimentón and stir in thoroughly.

Add the chicken stock, potatoes, and thyme and simmer for 20 minutes. Mash with a potato masher.

Blanch the spinach in boiling water for a matter of seconds, then refresh under cold running water. Finely chop it and add to the soup along with the crème fraîche or sour cream and some salt and black pepper.

This soup will store well in the refrigerator for a couple of days.

SERVES 4

5½ ounces chorizo, coarsely chopped

2 celery stalks, sliced

3 garlic cloves, chopped

1 medium onion, chopped

1 tablespoon olive oil

1 teaspoon picante pimentón (hot Spanish paprika)

2 cups plus heaping 1 tablespoon chicken stock

2 medium potatoes, diced

2 thyme sprigs

1 pound 2 ounces fresh spinach

1 heaping tablespoon crème fraîche or sour cream

salt and freshly ground black pepper

CASA RIERA ORDEIX: SPAIN

The small city of Vic in Catalunya is a sleepy sort of place. Its biggest moment in recent times was hosting the Roller Hockey tournament, which was one of the exhibition events at the 1992 Barcelona Olympics. Nevertheless, Vic is world famous for one thing: its air-dried sausages.

Since 1852, the definitive salchichon de Vic has been manufactured by Casa Riera Ordeix in the town's Plaza de los Martires (martyrs' square). When we arrived, we were convinced we had been given the wrong address. The building that purported to be the sausage factory was a town house with an elaborate sundial and a ceramic portrait of the eponymous saints on its facade. It looked like an upscale apartment block. The marbled lobby we found ourselves in after ringing the bell would have confirmed this impression had it not been for a large wooden device that resembled a medieval torture instrument. On closer inspection, it turned out to be a Victorian sausage stuffer.

After a few minutes, we were greeted by Jordi, the firm's commercial director, who was friendliness and enthusiasm personified. He ushered us into an opulent wood-paneled boardroom, where we donned the overalls required to be worn in the production area with the portraits of four generations of the Riera Ordeix family staring down at us. We were shortly joined by a living member of the fifth, the current proprietor Joaquim Comelia Benet. He has the bearing of a man who is used to moving in high places. Apparently, whenever King Alfonso XII (1875–85) visited Vic, he made a point of popping into the factory after meeting with the local bishop. Senor Joaquim didn't look as though he'd be fazed if Juan Carlos decided to revive the tradition.

The ground floor of the building is where the sausages are prepared and stuffed. Aside from an extraordinary glassed-off grotto housing a statue of the Madonna, it is as spick-and-span as any modern production facility. Jordi explained almost ruefully that the company had been forced to make changes to comply with European Union hygiene regulations. But although the surroundings are now thoroughly twenty-first century, the recipe for the salchichon de Vic is exactly as it was when the factory first opened its doors. There is no place for artificial preservatives or starter cultures. Just four ingredients are used: lean pork leg, cubes of bacon fat, salt, and black peppercorns. Having been mixed in the correct proportions, they are passed through a grinder and left to mature for 56 to 60 hours, whereupon they are stuffed into natural hog casings. It's that simple.

It is when the infant sausages are taken upstairs and back into the nineteenth century that the genius of Casa Riera Ordeix becomes apparent. The top four stories of the building, which have slatted floors to allow air to circulate freely, are filled with thousands of sausages hanging on wooden racks, usually in complete darkness. The five to six-month maturation process is controlled by two factors: moving the salchichon between stories according to their condition (the top floors are warmer due to hot air rising) and the strategic opening and closing of windows, with which the factory is equipped on all four sides.

The aim is to keep humidity within the building at a minimum of 80 percent. This effort is helped by Vic's foggy climate, which is the reason why the region has a sausage-making tradition in the first place. Nonetheless, the skill and judgment required of the firm's Master Curers are breathtaking. Everything must be done by instinct. A caretaker has to be on hand throughout the night in case the wind direction changes. If it does, he must immediately adjust the windows to ensure the factory's internal microclimate remains undisturbed. The main perk of this low-tech approach is that the workers get the summer off. There are no air-conditioning machines to fall back on, so production ceases during the hottest months of the year.

The sausages are made without starter cultures. There is no need for them after a century and a half—the desired microorganisms are part of the building's fabric. As a consequence, flavor-enhancing molds proliferate on the surfaces of the salchichon. They grow at such a rate that they have to be brushed off once a week—quite a task for one man with a tiny hand brush.

The sausages that emerge from this extended period of loving care resemble chorizos without the paprika. They have neat seams along the middle, betraying the fact that their skins are made by hand stitching two hog casings together. Anyone familiar with the slipperiness of natural casings will appreciate how difficult this must be to do, but barring the unthinkable (abandoning tradition by using other casings), there is no other way to produce salchichon with the required diameter.

The flavor of a finished salchichon de Vic has the depth and roundness of a top-notch salami, but with a firmer texture. The locals tend to cut the sausages into slices about ¼-inch thick and serve them on bread rubbed with chopped tomato and drizzled with olive oil. They are so good they need no other adornment. If you are lucky enough to get hold of the genuine article, keep it in a cool, airy place, but not in the refrigerator, or you may disrupt the balance of the internal microflora. Salut! as they say in Catalunya.

CHORIZO & GOAT CHEESE TART

Goat cheese goes particularly well with chorizo. You can roll out the pastry, make the filling, and bake this tart in less than an hour. Use a shallow, nonstick pizza pan with a ½-inch lip, approximately ½ inch deep and 11 inches across.

First make the pie dough. Sift the flour onto your counter. Cut the butter into pieces and place on top of the flour along with the cheese, salt, and nutmeg. Rub the ingredients together with the tips of your fingers until all the lumps of butter and cheese have melted into the mix. This will take a few minutes.

Make a well in the center of the mix and fill it with the yolks and egg white. Work the egg in with your fingers, then gather the pastry into a ball and work it with the heel of your hand for 30 seconds. Use the dough itself to mop up any loose bits that adhere to your counter. Work the dough again for a minute, then shape into a ball, wrap in plastic wrap, and store in the refrigerator until you need it (you can make the pie dough the day before you cook the tart).

When ready to make the tart, roll out the dough to the approximate size of the pizza pan, lay it over it, and press it down into the pan. Don't worry about trimming it around the side unless you feel the need strongly.

Preheat the oven to 475°F. Bake the bell pepper for 15 minutes, until charred, then let cool. Peel the skin away, remove the seeds, and slice the flesh into thin strips. Reduce the oven temperature to 400°F.

Mix the crème fraîche or sour cream, egg, thyme, and seasoning together with a fork or whisk. Spread the mixture onto the pie crust, making sure it goes all the way to the side. Sprinkle the goat cheese evenly on top, then lay over the roasted bell pepper strips in a haphazard manner, followed by the chorizo. Powder the surface with the pimentón and bake for 15 to 20 minutes, until the chorizo is nice and browned. Eat while still warm.

SERVES 3

The Pie Dough (enough for 1 tart)

¾ cup plus heaping 1 tablespoon all-purpose flour

¼ cup butter

¼ cup grated Parmesan cheese

dash of salt

a little grating of nutmeg

2 egg yolks from large eggs

½ white from a large egg

The Filling

1 large red bell pepper

½ cup crème fraîche or thick sour cream

1 large egg with 1 extra yolk

2 teaspoons chopped fresh thyme

salt and freshly ground black pepper

⅔ cup crumbled goat cheese

7 ounces fresh or cured chorizo, sliced or diced

¼ teaspoon pimentón or any other good-quality paprika, smoked or unsmoked (according to taste)

TORTILLA WITH SALCHICHON

SERVES 4

3½ ounces salchichon de Vic or
other cured sausage, thinly sliced,
then cut into narrow matchsticks

4 tablespoons olive oil

14 ounces small potatoes, thinly
sliced

2 medium red onions, sliced

4 garlic cloves, each sliced into
2 to 3 pieces

5 large eggs, lightly beaten

small bunch of flat-leaf parsley,
chopped

salt and freshly ground black pepper

scant 1 cup shredded Manchego
cheese

1 teaspoon pimentón (Spanish
paprika)

This tortilla uses the bold flavor of salchichon de Vic. If you don't
have any, feel free to use salami or any other cured sausage. You
will need a large nonstick skillet with a lid to cover the pan while the
potatoes cook.

Fry the salchichon in 1 tablespoon of the olive oil over medium heat
for 3 to 4 minutes, then remove from the pan with a slotted spoon
and set aside.

Add the remaining olive oil, the potatoes, red onions, and garlic and
gently fry with the lid on for 20 minutes, giving the pan an occasional
vigorous shake.

Preheat the broiler to its highest setting.

Add the eggs, salchichon, parsley, salt, and a little ground black pepper
to the potatoes and onions and stir them into the mixture.

Sprinkle the Manchego and pimentón on top and broil until golden
brown, about 5 minutes.

Serve with crusty bread and Rioja.

STIR-FRIED CHINESE SAUSAGES

Lap cheong need to be steamed prior to use as an ingredient. This is a quick and easy dish, best served with rice. You will need a wok and a steamer, although you can improvise the latter with a metal rack or colander set over a pan of boiling water.

——————————————————————————

Dry-roast the sesame seeds in a wok over medium heat until toasted, about 2 minutes.

Steam the lap cheong for 3 minutes and then coarsely slice them.

Stir-fry the ginger, scallions, greens, and Chinese sausages in the vegetable oil over quite a fierce heat for 3 to 4 minutes, tossing your wok continuously.

Turn off the heat and add the sesame oil and soy sauce.

Transfer to a dish and sprinkle with the toasted sesame seeds. Serve with steamed rice.

SERVES 2

2 teaspoons sesame seeds

4 lap cheong (Chinese sausages)

1½-inch piece fresh ginger, peeled and finely grated

5 scallions, sliced

3 heads of bok choy, choy sum, or other Chinese greens (or cabbage or spinach), sliced

1 tablespoon vegetable oil

1 tablespoon sesame oil

a shake of soy sauce

SESAME STEW WITH CHINESE SAUSAGES

SERVES 4

1 tablespoon sesame seeds

8 lap cheong (Chinese sausages)

sunflower oil, for frying

20 enoki, shiitake, or other Asian mushrooms

3 heads of bok choy, sliced

3 cups plus 2 tablespoons chicken stock

1½-inch piece fresh ginger, peeled and grated

5 scallions, sliced

1 tablespoon oyster sauce

2¼ cups cooked rice noodles

1 tablespoon soy sauce

sesame oil

Nick's wife is funny about food. She declares herself wheat and dairy free, but adores cream cakes. She is also a vegetarian sausage hater who loves lap cheong. She says this dish reminds her of her childhood in Guangzhao, where her family would purchase similar stews from a street hawker at a busy crossroads.

Toast the sesame seeds in a dry pan over medium heat until golden brown, about 2 minutes. Set aside.

Gently fry the Chinese sausages in 1 teaspoon sunflower oil, turning occasionally, until nicely browned. Set aside. (You may want to slice them before serving.)

While the sausages are frying, stir-fry the mushrooms and bok choy in 1 tablespoon sunflower oil in a wok for 3 to 5 minutes, tossing the ingredients frequently.

Add the chicken stock, ginger, scallions, oyster sauce, cooked rice noodles, soy sauce, and a good splash of sesame oil. Bring to a boil and serve immediately with the Chinese sausages and toasted sesame seeds.

SKINLESS SAUSAGES & SAUSAGE MEAT

You don't always have to go through the rigmarole of filling ingredients into casings to enjoy the flavors and textures associated with sausages. One of our favorite parts of the process of making them is frying a little patty of sausage meat before we commit to stuffing it into casings, to test the seasoning. The real point of a sausage, after all, is the mixture it is stuffed with. The qualities that make a good sausage filling—judicious seasoning, toothsome balance between fat and lean meat, and so on— frequently make it an excellent cooking ingredient in its own right. Sausage meat makes an excellent stuffing for roasts, as we hope this chapter proves. It is also the basis for classic snacks such as Scotch eggs and sausage rolls, which haven't been anywhere near animal intestines.

HERBY SAUSAGE DUMPLINGS IN ROOT VEGETABLE STEW

This warming stew is very versatile—you can make the sausage dumplings with any meat you fancy, though ideally it should have a little fat in it.

━━━━━━━━━━━━━━━━━

In a large bowl, mix all the dumpling ingredients together, except the olive oil, for a few minutes, then form the mixture into about 12 golf-ball-size dumplings.

Heat a nonstick skillet and fry the dumplings in the olive oil over medium heat for a couple of minutes on each side until browned. Take off the heat and reserve in the pan with all the juices.

To make the stew, slowly fry the onion, carrot, and celery in the butter with the lid on the pan, stirring occasionally.

Add the chicken stock, potatoes, parsnip, and rutabaga and simmer until the vegetables are cooked, about 30 minutes.

Add the leek and dumplings with their juices and simmer for another 10 minutes.

Stir in the cream or crème fraîche and parsley and serve in large bowls.

SERVES 4

The Dumplings

1 pound 2 ounces ground pork, lamb, or beef

2 small shallots, finely chopped

2 to 3 thyme sprigs, chopped

4 fresh sage leaves and 2 large flat-leaf parsley sprigs, finely chopped

scant 1 teaspoon salt and 1½ teaspoons black pepper

½ nutmeg, grated

2 teaspoons olive oil, for frying

The Stew

1 onion and 1 large carrot, peeled and coarsely chopped

2 celery stalks, sliced

1 tablespoon butter

heaping 3 cups chicken stock

2 medium potatoes, peeled and diced

2 parsnips, peeled and sliced

½ small rutabaga, peeled and diced

1 medium leek, washed and sliced

⅓ cup plus heaping 1 tablespoon heavy cream or crème fraîche

handful of flat-leaf parsley, chopped

SAUSAGE PASTIES

MAKES 8 PASTIES

1 egg, lightly beaten

The Filling

12 robust fresh sausages

2 teaspoons vegetable oil

1 tablespoon olive oil

1¾ ounces smoked pancetta, diced

heaping 1 tablespoon unsalted butter

1 medium carrot, peeled and diced

2 medium shallots, diced

½ fennel bulb, diced

1 tablespoon all-purpose flour

¾ cup plus heaping 1 tablespoon chicken stock

heaping 1 cup red wine

salt and freshly ground black pepper

The Pie Dough

1¾ cups all-purpose flour, plus extra for dusting

½ teaspoon salt

⅓ cup butter

⅓ cup shortening, shredded

The pasty was invented by tin miners in Cornwall, Southwest England, who didn't want to contaminate their lunches with arsenic, which was present in high levels in the mines. They held their pasties by the pastry "crimps," which were discarded once they had eaten the rest of the pockets. Pasties are traditionally filled with a mixture of beef, potato, and onion. Had the good folk of Cornwall tried stuffing them with top-quality sausages, the story might have been different.

Fry the sausages in the vegetable oil in large pan over low heat for 15 minutes, then remove them from the pan. When they are cool enough to handle, slice them up and set aside. Pour the olive oil into the pan, add the pancetta, butter, carrot, shallots, and fennel, and fry gently for 8 to 10 minutes. Spoon in the flour and mix it in until you can't see it anymore. Pour in a little of the stock and stir it in. The mixture will become thick and gluey. Add a bit more stock, stir it in, and then pour in the rest along with the red wine and the sliced sausages. Simmer for 15 minutes, add salt and pepper if you like, and let cool.

To make the pie dough, sift the flour into a large bowl and add the salt. Add the butter and shortening and rub them into the flour using the tips of your fingers. Slowly pour cold water into the bowl, squeezing and manipulating the flour-and-butter mixture as you do so, until you have a stiff dough. Turn out the dough onto a counter lightly dusted with flour and knead with the heel of your hand for a minute or two. Roll the dough into a ball, cover it with plastic wrap, and store it in the refrigerator until needed.

When you're ready to make the pasties, preheat the oven to 400°F. Roll the dough into a long sausage and divide it into 8 sections. Then roll each section into a ball. Take one of your balls of dough and roll it into a circle about 6 inches in diameter. Place 3 to 3½ ounces of sausage filling in the center of the circle and paint beaten egg around its perimeter. Then pull up the sides of the pastry and press the seams together to form a neat, pasty-shaped pocket. Repeat the procedure 7 times, then paint the outside of the pasties with the remaining beaten egg and bake them on a greased baking sheet or silicone sheet for 10 minutes. At this point, reduce the oven temperature to 350°F and continue to bake for 25 to 30 minutes, until golden brown.

SAUSAGE CANNELLONI

SERVES 4

The Cannelloni

1⅔ cups durum wheat flour ("semolato di grano duro")

2 large eggs, weighing 5 ounces in total

1¾ pounds sausage meat

The Sauce

2 cups plus heaping 1 tablespoon milk

1 medium leek, washed and sliced

1 small red onion, sliced

3 tablespoons butter

scant 3 tablespoons all-purpose flour

⅓ cup plus heaping 1 tablespoon crème fraîche or thick sour cream

scant 1 cup shredded cheddar cheese

salt and freshly ground black pepper

The Topping

½ cup shredded cheddar cheese

These succulent tubes of sausage meat will taste best if you make your own sheets of pasta, but you can always buy some in—if so you will need about 16 sheets of fresh pasta. You can use any sausage meat you like for the stuffing—we'd recommend the mixture used to make fresh paysanne on page 15.

If you want to make the pasta yourself, place the flour in a pile on your counter and make a well in the center. Break the eggs into this well. Whisk them gently, gradually adding more flour from the rim of the well until all the egg is incorporated. Work the mixture with your fingers into a sticky mass and continue until it becomes smooth. It is important that you use up all the flour. Check to see whether the dough is of the right consistency. Stick your thumb in. If it comes out clean, the dough is ready. Knead the dough with the heel of your hand, half turning it as you go (always in the same direction). Knead for at least 5 minutes. Divide into 3 parts and follow the instructions on your pasta machine or roll out the dough thinly.

Your sheets of pasta (homemade or store-bought) should be about 4 to 4½ inches long. You can then cut them into widths about 3¼ inches.

To make the sauce, slowly heat the milk up in a pan, making sure it doesn't come to a boil.

In the meantime, gently fry the leek and onion in the butter until soft, about 10 minutes, then stir in the flour. Slowly add the hot milk, stirring as you go. Add the crème fraîche or sour cream and cheddar, and season to taste. Simmer for 5 minutes, stirring frequently. Take off the heat and cover the sauce with a sheet of wax paper to prevent a skin forming. Set aside until you've prepared the cannelloni.

To do this, roll up approximately 1¾ ounces of sausage meat in each rectangle of pasta.

Preheat the oven to 350°F.

Pour a little of the sauce into an oven dish and lay a single layer of cannelloni on top. Pour on some more sauce, add the rest of the cannelloni, and cover with the remaining sauce.

Sprinkle the shredded cheddar on top and bake for 20 minutes. Now ramp up the heat to 425°F and bake for 5 minutes more. Serve with a pile of cooked spinach and some chunky bread.

CORN DOGS

1 pound 5 ounces finely ground pork

1 teaspoon salt

1 teaspoon ground white pepper

heaping ½ teaspoon ground mace

2 teaspoons Colman's mustard powder

1 slice of fresh processed white bread, blended into fine bread crumbs in a food processor

1 tablespoon dried mixed herbs

¾ cup polenta

oil, for deep-frying

Like many fast-food items, corn dogs, an American staple, are not always made of the finest ingredients—a typical example is a big glob of mechanically recovered sausage meat surrounded by fat-infused crispy batter—but even street corn dogs can taste fantastic, especially when dipped in ketchup. This is a healthier version with a crunchy polenta crust. You will need a 1½ to 2½-inch round cookie cutter and some wooden skewers.

Place the ground pork in a large bowl. Add the salt, pepper, mace, mustard powder, and bread crumbs. Mix with your fingers until you have a big gloopy mass.

Mix the herbs with the polenta and then sprinkle a light layer of the mix onto your counter.

Place the meat patty onto this layer and flatten it into a sheet around ½ inch thick.

Sprinkle with as much of the polenta mix as will stick and then cut out circles with a 1½ to 2-inch round cookie cutter. Before you remove the cutter, cut around the edges with a knife so you're not left with unsightly strands of meat.

Thread the circles onto wooden skewers.

Heat oil for deep-frying in a wok to the point at which a wooden kebab stick sizzles when inserted into it, then fry the corn dogs until thoroughly crispy, 3 to 4 minutes.

Serve with squirts of tomato ketchup.

CHORIZO DOG

SERVES 1

1 fresh chorizo

½ red bell pepper, seeded

1 length of crusty baguette

This recipe is ideal for cooking on the grill or frying on a grill pan. At Borough Market in Southeast London, our friends Brindisa serve similar "dogs" in crusty bread with Piquillo peppers. The lines are endless.

— — — — — — — — — — — — — —

First you will need to butterfly the chorizo: cut it down the middle lengthwise and splay it face down.

Cook the chorizo and bell pepper for about 5 minutes on each side. If you are using a grill, place the bell pepper over the hottest area and the chorizo over a cooler area. Watch it doesn't catch fire—the fat has a tendency to ignite!

While the chorizo and bell pepper are cooking, slice the baguette in half lengthwise and warm it either toward the side of the grill or under a broiler.

Place the chorizo and bell pepper inside the bread and tuck in.

CHORIZO RAVIOLI WITH PARSLEY SAUCE

If you've never made your own pasta before, you could do much worse than start with these ravioli, which are served in a zesty parsley sauce. Just bear in mind that it is important that you get the quantities right. Full instructions are given below but, if you lack time or energy, you can always buy sheets of fresh pasta.

To make the pasta, place the flour in a pile on your counter and make a well in the center. Break the eggs into this well. Whisk them gently, gradually adding more flour from the rim of the well until all the egg is incorporated. Work with your fingers into a sticky mass and continue until it becomes smooth. It is important that you use up all the flour. Check to see whether the dough is of the right consistency. Stick your thumb in. If it comes out clean, the dough is ready. Knead the dough with the heel of your hand, half turning it as you go (always in the same direction). Knead for at least 5 minutes. Divide into 3 parts and follow the instructions on your pasta machine or roll out thinly.

Mix together the ingredients for the chorizo filling in a bowl until firm and sticky. Set aside.

Take a round cutter that's about 2 to 2½ inches in diameter and cut the pasta dough into 40 circles. This will give you with 20 ravioli, 5 for each diner. Thoroughly egg wash 20 of the pasta circles and place a heaped teaspoon of chorizo filling in the center of each one. Cover with an un-egged circle and press down from the center outward to remove any air pockets. Then seal the edges of the circles by pressing them together with a fingertip.

Bring a large pan of water to a boil, simmer the ravioli for 5 minutes, then drain and dress with a drizzle of olive oil. While the ravioli are cooking, melt the butter in a small skillet over medium heat until it stops bubbling and starts to turn amber. Pour in the lemon juice, making the butter fizz up. Add some black pepper and the parsley and immediately pour over the drained and dressed ravioli. Season with a little salt and freshly ground black pepper, and serve.

SERVES 4

1 egg, lightly beaten

olive oil, for dressing

salt and freshly ground black pepper

The Pasta

1⅔ cups durum wheat flour ("semolato di grano duro")

2 large eggs, weighing 5 ounces in total

The Filling

9 ounces pork belly, ground

1 cup freshly blended white bread crumbs

1 tablespoon plus 1½ teaspoons Pimentón de la Vera

2 garlic cloves, chopped

¾ teaspoon salt

The Sauce

¼ cup unsalted butter

juice of 1 lemon

freshly ground black pepper

¾ cup chopped flat-leaf parsley

SAUSAGE ROLLS WITH ONION CONFIT

MAKES 12

The Filling

1 pound 5 ounces finely ground pork belly or pork (picnic) shoulder (needs to be about 20 percent fat otherwise it will taste too dry)

1¾ teaspoons salt

small flat-leaf parsley sprig, chopped

6 fresh sage leaves, chopped

3 thyme sprigs, chopped

1 teaspoon cracked black pepper

3 garlic cloves, chopped

The Rolls

confit of onion or onion chutney

tomato ketchup

9 ounces puff pastry, thinly rolled out and cut into 3¼ to 4-inch squares

These sausage rolls are easy to make and have a tempting balance of sweet and savory flavors.

Mix the filling ingredients in a large bowl until sticky and glutinous.

On each square of pastry place ½ teaspoon onion confit or chutney, a chipolata-size blob of sausage-meat filling, and a small squiggle of ketchup. Form into a reasonably tight cylindrical roll, squeezing the edges of the dough together. Cut 2 diagonal slashes on the top of the roll, then repeat the procedure until you have used up all the ingredients.

Preheat the oven to 350°F.

Bake the rolls for 20 minutes, until golden brown. Serve with tomato ketchup.

SCOTCH EGGS

SERVES 4

1 pound 5 ounces pork, finely ground (coarsely ground meat won't hold together)

1.8 ounces finely blended fresh bread crumbs

1¼ teaspoons salt

1½ teaspoons freshly ground black pepper

heaping ½ teaspoon ground mace

½ teaspoon ground cardamom

6 boiled eggs (boil them from cold; once up to temperature, boil for 7 minutes, then refresh under cold running water and peel)

all-purpose flour, for coating

1 egg, beaten

7 ounces coarsely blended bread crumbs, made from fresh bread with a good texture

oil, for deep-frying

If ever a food needed rehabilitation, it is the once not-so-humble Scotch egg. Invented by Fortnum & Mason in 1738, it has become horribly degraded in the form of inexpensive mass-produced versions, but by making your own you can help restore this picnic delicacy to its former glory. We fry our Scotch eggs in a large wok.

In a large bowl, mix together the ground pork, the finely blended bread crumbs, salt, pepper, mace, and cardamom. If you have latex gloves (a must for sausage-making enthusiasts), don a pair and do it with your fingers. Divide the mixture into 6 balls.

Coat a peeled egg in flour. Flatten a ball of sausage meat and carefully squeeze it around the egg.

Roll the ball in flour, dip it into the beaten egg, and finally roll it in the coarsely blended bread crumbs.

Repeat this process with the rest of the eggs.

Heat the oil to 320°F in a wok and fry the Scotch eggs until golden brown, 8 to 10 minutes.

Serve with mustard mayonnaise or piccalilli.

ROASTED GOOSE WITH VEAL STUFFING

SERVES 6

3½ ounces bacon, chopped

2¼ pounds ground veal

9 ounces cooked peeled sweet chestnuts, chopped (either prepare them yourself by broiling them for 10 minutes or use ready-prepared cooked whole chestnuts)

10 fresh sage leaves, chopped

1 cup coarsely chopped onion

2 cups fresh white bread crumbs

excess fat from the goose (see below), chopped

1 teaspoon ground mace

generous grating of nutmeg

small bunch of flat-leaf parsley, chopped

3 thyme sprigs, chopped

fine or flaky salt and freshly ground black pepper

1 large goose weighing 10 pounds to 12 pounds 2 ounces (including giblets), trimmed of excess fat (which should be used in the stuffing)

½ bottle red wine

For this luxurious recipe you will need a goose weighing around 11 pounds (including the giblets), trimmed of any excess fat. Don't throw it away, though—you'll need it for the stuffing.

Preheat the oven to 350°F.

To make the stuffing, in a large bowl, mix together the bacon, veal, chestnuts, sage, onion, bread crumbs, excess fat from the goose, mace, nutmeg, parsley, thyme, 1 teaspoon fine or flaky salt, and lots of black pepper. Stuff the goose with the mixture, lightly pushing it into the body cavity.

Rub the bird with salt and pepper, then place it in a roasting pan and roast it for 2½ hours.

Remove the goose from the oven and place it on a cutting board. Let the bird rest for at least 20 minutes before you touch it.

While the goose is resting, make the gravy. There will be a good deal of excess fat from the goose left in the roasting pan. Pour this off, then pour the wine into the roasting pan and place it on your stovetop. Gently heat until the wine boils. Reduce by half, stirring and scraping as you go to dissolve all the flavorsome encrustations.

This recipe cries out for braised red cabbage, roast potatoes, and apple or gooseberry sauce as accompaniments.

ROLLED PORK LOIN WITH RUSTIC SAUSAGE STUFFING

For this stunning recipe you need to use what is known as pork tenderloin. This consists of the belly and loin together in one piece. Ask your butcher for a boned section weighing about 4½ pounds and get him to score the skin for you. You will need some butcher twine and a roasting pan with a rack.

- -

Mix the ingredients for the stuffing together in a large bowl. Cover with plastic wrap and store in the refrigerator until ready to use.

Lay the pork tenderloin flat on a large plate or baking sheet skin-side up and cover in a thin layer of salt. Rub the salt deep into the cracks and leave for 2 hours. At the end of this period, wash the salt off thoroughly and pat the meat dry.

Preheat the oven to 475°F.

Turn the meat over so the skin side is on the counter.

Mold the stuffing into a thick sausage and press it into the nook between the "eye" of the loin and the belly section.

Roll the meat up tightly and tie with string in at least 4 places. Place the knots at the bottom where the extremities of the pork tenderloin overlap.

Pour a little olive oil into a bowl and add the dried sage and rosemary. Season with salt and pepper and rub the mixture over the outside of the pork roll with your fingers.

Place the roll on a rack over a roasting pan—this will make sure it crisps up nicely all over—and roast for 20 minutes, then reduce the heat to 350°F and continue roasting for 1 hour 40 minutes. Serve with roast potatoes and braised cabbage.

SERVES 4 to 6

The Roast

4½ pounds pork tenderloin

fine sea salt and freshly ground black pepper

olive oil

1 teaspoon dried sage

1 teaspoon dried rosemary

The Stuffing

2 thyme sprigs, chopped

10 fresh sage leaves

small bunch of flat-leaf parsley, chopped

4 garlic cloves, chopped

2 teaspoons hot paprika

1 teaspoon fennel seeds

2 teaspoons coarsely ground black pepper

⅓ cup plus heaping 1 tablespoon red wine

2¼ pounds coarsely ground fatty pork

SAUSAGE COUSINS

Not everything that is stuffed into an animal casing is best described as a sausage. Haggis falls into this category, as do crepinettes and faggots. Blood puddings certainly look like sausages, but are sufficiently different from orthodox varieties to squeeze into this chapter. They also illustrate the point that cousins of the sausage tend not to be for the fainthearted. Blood, sheep's lungs, and the like won't appeal to everyone, but we hope the recipes that follow will tempt you to set aside any preconceptions. Some of the most prominent "sausage cousins" depend on ingredients and techniques beyond the scope of the average home sausage maker. We're not about to teach you how to make andouillettes, for example, but we can certainly show you some good things to do with them.

BLACK PUDDING WITH CAULIFLOWER, TOPPED WITH ROASTED HAZELNUTS

This recipe is suitable for any kind of black pudding, including continental varieties such as morcilla or boudin noir. You can also make a good version with haggis. Whatever kind of sausage you use, you will end up with a dish that was easy to throw together but looks most attractive.

3 tablespoons hazelnuts

1 large cauliflower

14 ounces black pudding (blood sausage), crumbled or sliced

1¼ cups crème fraîche or thick sour cream

1 cup grated Parmesan cheese

4 sprigs rosemary

Preheat the oven to 350°F. Roast the hazelnuts for 6 minutes, then coarsely chop them or give them a couple of seconds in the blender. Set aside. Leave the oven on.

Meanwhile, break the cauliflower into florets and blanch them in boiling water for a couple of minutes. Drain and pour into an oven dish.

Add the sausage, mix in the crème fraîche or sour cream, then sprinkle the Parmesan over the top.

Stick the rosemary sprigs deep into the cauliflower–black pudding mixture and sprinkle with the chopped hazelnuts.

Bake in the oven for 30 minutes, until golden brown.

CRISPY ANDOUILLE WITH FIVE-SPICE

**MAKES I SMALL BOWL
OF CRISPY ANDOUILLE**

15 thin slices of andouille

½ teaspoon five-spice powder

1 teaspoon teriyaki sauce

vegetable oil, for deep frying

The andouille de Guémené, from the Loire Valley in France, is a strange-looking sausage; each slice is a visual feast of tightly packed, ever decreasing concentric circles. Made from chitterlings, the construction of this sausage is an art form. Many years ago, the *Confrerie de Chevaliers du Goutte-andouille* was formed as the guardian of this artisan process. Sadly, the society has now been disbanded after the death of its revered master. Never tell a Frenchman that you're going to fry your andouille. He'll murder you! Once they are fried they look like golden, whirling gnome's hats, at least if you are feeling sufficiently whimsical.

Coat the andouille in the spice and teryaki sauce.

Heat the oil to around 340°F. Fry the andouille until golden brown, about 2 minutes, then place on paper towels to soak up the excess oil. Serve with sweet chilli sauce.

WARM SALAD WITH SAUTÉ POTATOES & BLACK PUDDING

Black pudding has an ambiguous reputation in Britain. On the one hand, it is a staple of transport cafés, "greasy spoons," and the like—places not always renowned for their culinary excellence. On the other, it is increasingly popular in high-class restaurants, where its versatility is much appreciated (it goes particularly well with seafood and roast meats). This dish would be more at home in the latter than the former. It works equally well with English-style black pudding, French boudin noir, and Spanish morcilla (although morcilla tends to break up in the pan).

Make the dressing in a medium bowl. Add the garlic and vinegar to the egg yolk and briefly whisk. Pour in the olive oil very, very slowly, whisking as you go, to create a thick dressing. Finish off with a squeeze of lemon juice and a dash of salt.

Cut the potatoes into cubes, boil them for 10 minutes, and drain. Then fry them in a large pan in olive oil over medium heat until nicely browned, about 10 minutes. Set aside.

Remove the potatoes and pour off any excess oil. Fry the pancetta and the black pudding, boudin noir, or morcilla for a couple of minutes on each side.

In a large bowl, toss the pancetta and black pudding, boudin noir, or morcilla with the potatoes and watercress. Decorate the salad with blobs of glistening dressing and serve.

SERVES 2

2 to 3 medium potatoes, unpeeled

2 tablespoons olive oil

4 thin slices of smoked pancetta

6 slices of black pudding, boudin noir, or morcilla

bunch of washed watercress (weighing about 2¾ to 3½ ounces)

The Dressing

1 garlic clove, finely chopped

2 teaspoons sherry vinegar

1 egg yolk

⅓ cup plus heaping 1 tablespoon olive oil

squeeze of lemon juice

salt

MCSWEEN: SCOTLAND

The dish that Rabbie Burns described as "chieftain of the pudding race" is a subject of fascination for the rest of the world. It isn't just theoretical either—thanks to the effort of the marketing industry, Burns Night (January 25), on which haggis is ritually consumed along with excessive quantities of whisky, has become a fixture way beyond the boundaries of Scotland. Whether you live in Sydney or Tokyo, there is a fair chance that this delicacy will make it to your plate sooner or later. You might as well know how it's made.

To find out the answer, we traveled to the Edinburgh suburb of Loanhead, home of McSween, the world's biggest manufacturer of naturally cased haggis. The walk from the bus stop to the factory was bracing in the extreme—this was Scotland in February after all, and the hills on the horizon were sprinkled with snow—but we soon warmed up once inside the state-of-the-art facility. We were met by Jo McSween (the "haggis queen"), a granddaughter of the company's founders, who runs the business together with her brother James. Jo is a feisty, quick-witted lady. When we had the temerity to point out that she didn't have much of a Scottish accent, she immediately responded that she toned it down so her English customers could understand her.

Traditionally, as Jo explained, the basis of a haggis was the "pluck" of a sheep—in other words, the lungs, heart, liver, and spleen. McSween, however, only use the lungs, or "lites" as they are known in Scotland. The other organs are considered too iron-ish and pungent. Another advantage of sticking to the lungs is the light, airy quality they give to the finished "chieftains." This is no great surprise when you consider their job in the living sheep. Jo showed us a huge container of raw lites. They had a pleasantly fresh aroma and definitely came from sheep who were nonsmokers. Only the lobes are used—the tracheas are discarded.

The one drawback with lites is that they contain zero fat. This would make the haggises unpalatably chewy, so they are mixed with beef suet obtained from what Jo described as cows' "love handles." The other key ingredients are two grades of oatmeal (pinhead and medium), which give the end products their distinctive texture, kibbled onion, which is preferred to the fresh version as there are fewer contamination issues, and a secret blend of spices. Jo was too smart to divulge the formula, but she did admit that ground coriander seed and black pepper were among the components.

Back in the old days, the haggis mixture would be stuffed into sheep's stomachs, but this tradition has now lapsed. This is partly because the skills involved in preparing stomachs for this purpose have been forgotten and partly because a haggis made this way would weigh at least 6½ pounds, which is impractical, given the reduced size of today's households. McSween now use beef bungs, which are made from the widest part of a cow's large intestine. They have to be bought in from South America and need to be soaked for two days to remove the salt in which they are packed.

Each bung is slightly different in shape, which gives a pleasing variety to the finished haggises.

As we walked through the factory, we saw the various processes involved in haggis making in action. First, the lites and fat are boiled for a couple of hours and passed twice through a grinder. Next, the oats, onions, and seasonings are added to the mixture, which is then stuffed into the beef bungs. These are sealed with aluminum clips, leaving little "ears" of unstuffed casing that make the young haggises look like living creatures. The chieftains are then steam-cooked for an hour (a procedure that invariably produces a few casualties, whose skins burst as their contents expand), cooled, and blast-chilled. Finally, the ears are removed with a knife and the haggises are vacuum-packed, which gives them a five-week shelf life.

On our departure, we were each presented with a haggis, a vegetarian version, and a pack of microwavable haggis slices, a new line about which Jo is very excited. We had worked up quite an appetite by now, so we headed into Edinburgh for lunch at the Whiski Bar in the Royal Mile. Naturally we ordered the "haggis tower," made with puddings from McSween's. It took the form of a mound of buttered mashed potato and rutabaga (neeps) with a haggis dome in a sea of thick, whisky-infused gravy. It was a highly savory dish with a lovely range of textures, which quickly dispelled any lingering "Sassenach" (i.e. English person's) anxiety about eating haggis.

A final word of warning: if you make or buy a haggis, don't be tempted to eat the casing. It should be discarded as soon as you have released the steaming contents.

HAGGIS, NEEPS & TATTIES

This is a slightly updated version of the classic Burns Night supper. Traditionally minded Scots might balk at the crème fraîche and parsley in the vegetables but we think they improve the time-honored formula.

Cover the haggis with foil and place it in a pan, then cover with water, put the lid on, and simmer for 40 minutes.

Meanwhile, cook the rutabaga and potatoes in separate pots of boiling water and cook until soft, around 30 minutes, then drain.

For the neeps, mash the rutabaga with the butter, crème fraîche or sour cream, milk, salt, and white pepper.

For the tatties, mash the potatoes with the butter, crème fraîche or sour cream, milk, parsley, salt, and white pepper.

Break open the haggis and serve everything together, preferably in a thick, whisky-enriched gravy.

SERVES 2 to 3

1 x 1 pound 2 ounce haggis

The Neeps

1 rutabaga, peeled and coarsely chopped

2 tablespoons butter

3 tablespoons crème fraîche or thick sour cream

3 tablespoons milk

salt and ground white pepper

The Tatties

5 medium potatoes, peeled and coarsely chopped

2 tablespoons butter

3 tablespoons crème fraîche or thick sour cream

3 tablespoons milk

small flat-leaf parsley sprig, chopped

salt and ground white pepper

CREPINETTES WITH SPINACH & ROASTED ALMONDS

SERVES 4

1 medium butternut squash, peeled, seeded, and coarsely sliced

1 tablespoon olive oil

salt and freshly ground black pepper

½ cup slivered almonds

1 pound 2 ounces caul fat, softened in tepid water for about 1 hour

½ quantity sausage meat from Nick's Chipolatas recipe (see page 16)

14 ounces baby spinach leaves

Crepinettes are packages of sausage meat wrapped in caul fat, a delicate, lacy membrane that surrounds a mammal's internal organs. Caul fat fat comes in thin sheets and can be bought from traditional butchers.

Preheat the oven to 400°F. Toss the squash in the olive oil and salt and pepper to taste in a roasting pan. Bake for 35 minutes, until soft and browned. Put the almonds in an oven dish and pop them into the oven for the last 5 minutes of the cooking time. Set aside.

Peel off thin layers of caul fat and cut into eight 4-inch squares. Place 3½ ounces sausage meat in the center of each square and wrap into a neat package, trimming off any excess fat. Shape each package into a thick patty and fry in a large nonstick skillet or flat-bottomed wok over medium heat for 6 to 8 minutes on each side. Add the squash, stir in the spinach, and, once it wilts, transfer everything to warmed plates. Garnish with the slivered almonds. Serve with hot crusty bread.

FAGGOT & ROOT VEGETABLE STEW

The Faggots

1 pound 2 ounces caul fat

1 pound 5 ounces finely ground pork belly or pork (picnic) shoulder

1¾ teaspoons salt and 1 teaspoon cracked black pepper

1 parsley sprig, 6 fresh sage leaves, and 3 thyme sprigs, chopped

3 garlic cloves, chopped

The Stew

3 medium leeks, washed and coarsely chopped

6 slices of bacon, sliced

1 medium onion, sliced

¼ cup butter

⅔ cup white wine

1¼ cups chicken stock

4 medium potatoes, thinly sliced

4 fresh sage leaves, chopped

½ nutmeg, grated

⅓ cup plus heaping 1 tablespoon crème fraîche or thick sour cream

salt and freshly ground black pepper

Faggots are essentially British crepinettes (see page 172)—both are made by wrapping ground meat in caul fat (available from traditional butchers). Known colloquially as "ducks" in their native English Midlands, faggots are often made with liver, hearts, and other internal organs. This version omits the variety meats, resulting in a lighter, less metallic flavor. You will need pork belly or shoulder for this, ideally with a fat content of around 20 to 25 percent.

Before you start, soften the caul fat in tepid water for an hour or so.

To make the faggots, in a large bowl, mix together the ground pork, salt, pepper, herbs, and garlic.

Peel off thin layers of caul fat and cut into six 4-inch squares. Place 3½ ounces of sausage meat in the center of each square and wrap it up into a package. Trim away any excess fat. Shape each package into a ball.

Fry the faggots over medium heat in a large skillet for 6 to 8 minutes on each side. Set aside.

Gently fry the leeks, bacon, and onion in the butter in a large pan for 20 minutes, stirring frequently.

Add the wine, chicken stock, potatoes, chopped sage leaves, and grated nutmeg. Simmer for 3 minutes, then add the faggots and simmer for another 10 minutes.

Spoon in the crème fraîche or sour cream, season with salt and pepper, and serve.

BLACK PUDDING WITH APPLE & FIG

Fruit goes really well with black pudding—the acidity of the fruit cuts through the unctuousness of the pudding to delightful effect. This appetizer is as visually appealing as it is tasty.

Core and slice the apple, then gently fry it with the onion in the butter, sugar, and vinegar until gooey and caramelized, about 20 minutes. Add the mustard and cream, then transfer to a small bowl.

Wipe the pan clean and pour in the olive oil. Fry the black pudding over medium heat for a couple of minutes on each side until crispy.

Place a scoop of onion and apple mix on each plate. Top with 2 slices of black pudding, laying a quarter of a fig on each slice, and serve.

SERVES 2

1 rosy apple (preferably Braeburn, Jonagold, or Golden Delicious)

1 red onion, sliced

1 tablespoon butter

2 teaspoons sugar

2 teaspoons cider vinegar

1 teaspoon Dijon mustard

1 tablespoon heavy cream

1 tablespoon olive oil

4 slices of black pudding

1 ripe fresh fig, quartered

FISH & VEGGIE SAUSAGES

There is no escaping the fact that sausages are associated with meat in most people's minds, but it would be a great mistake to think the story ends there. When all is said and done, a sausage is something encased in something else and there is no law that states either of the somethings must come from animals. Writing this chapter and eating the results has been a revelation to your thoroughly carnivorous authors. The late Linda McCartney had a point: vegetarian sausages can be just as good as meat-based ones. The operative word is succulence. Sealing fish, mushrooms, or vegetables in a casing guarantees this quality in abundance. The only price vegetarians have to pay is that cellulose casings are not suitable for frying.

SMOKED MACKEREL BOUDIN

1 pound 10 ounces smoked mackerel, skin removed, broken into pieces

½ cup chopped flat-leaf parsley

2⅓ cups crème fraîche or thick sour cream

2 teaspoons ground white pepper

scant 1 teaspoon salt

3 large eggs

1.8 ounces fresh white bread crumbs

1¾ yards collagen or hog casings

2 teaspoons butter (optional)

Finely puréed mackerel sets into a beautiful pâté in these simple sausages. You can make them with either collagen or natural casings. Serve the boudin with horseradish sauce and a beet salad.

Heat up a large pan of water.

Blend together the smoked mackerel, parsley, crème fraîche or sour cream, pepper, salt, eggs, and bread crumbs in a food processor until smooth. Stuff the mix into your casings, then tie off well and twist into sausages.

Blanch the boudins at 176 to 185°F for 20 minutes if you are using collagen casings, or 30 minutes for hog ones. Remove the sausages from the pan, chill them under cold running water, and set aside. You can store them in the refrigerator for up to 3 days, or freeze them until you need them (but don't freeze for longer than 6 months).

If you've made your boudins in advance, you'll need to thaw them, if frozen, and reheat them before serving. If they have collagen casings, gently heat them in water for 10 minutes. If you used hog casings, fry them very slowly in the butter for around 20 minutes.

Serve with horseradish sauce and a crunchy salad with grated raw beets and pea shoots or corn salad.

TOFU SAUSAGES WITH SHIITAKE MUSHROOMS

MAKES 20 to 25
CHIPOLATA-SIZE
SAUSAGES

1 cup sesame seeds

½ cup cilantro, chopped

7 ounces chopped shiitake
mushrooms

1 cup scallions, chopped

1 pound 2 ounces fresh tofu, diced

scant ½ cup peeled fresh ginger,
finely chopped

scant ½ cup miso paste

⅓ cup plus 1 tablespoon and
1 teaspoon teriyaki sauce

3 tablespoons plus 1 teaspoon
sesame oil

3 tablespoons plus 1 teaspoon
vegetable oil

1 pound 2 ounces cooked
glutinous rice

small spool of sheep casings or
cellulose casings

2 teaspoons sunflower oil (optional)

Not being vegetarians, we make these splendid sausages with sheep casings. If this doesn't appeal, you can use cellulose ones, but then you'll have to warm up the sausages by boiling rather than frying them.

Dry-fry the sesame seed gently, tossing them frequently, until golden brown, about 10 minutes.

In a large bowl, combine all the ingredients, except the casings and sunflower oil, and mix until mushy using a spoon or your fingers.

Fill into your chosen casings and tie off into chipolata-length sausages.

Simmer the sausages at 158 to 176°F for 40 minutes. Don't let the water temperature get any higher or the casings may split.

Cool the sausages under cold running water. They will keep in the refrigerator for up to 5 days, or in the freezer for up to 6 months.

When the time comes to eat them, thaw them if frozen and fry them very gently in the oil in a nonstick pan until browned (if you made them with sheep casings), or simmer them until warmed through (if you used cellulose casings).

Serve with stir-fried Chinese greens.

BACALAO & PARSLEY SAUSAGES

Bacalao is salted cod, which has to be soaked prior to use. As with our Tofu Sausages with Shiitake Mushrooms (see opposite), you can use either sheep or cellulose casings, but if you go for the latter, you won't be able to fry them ahead of serving. You'll have to blanch them instead.

Drain the bacalao and pat dry with paper towels. Gently fry the bacalao, shallots, and garlic in the olive oil for 15 minutes, stirring frequently.

Transfer to your food processor along with the flat-leaf parsley, eggs, pimentón, crème fraîche or sour cream, and potatoes. Pulse about 10 times until mixed.

Fill into your chosen casings and tie off into chipolata-length sausages.

Simmer the sausages at 158 to 176°F for 40 minutes. Don't let the water temperature get any higher or the casings may split.

Cool the sausages under cold running water. They will keep in the refrigerator for up to 5 days, or in the freezer for up to 6 months.

When you're ready to eat them, fry them very gently in the butter in a nonstick pan until browned (if you made them with sheep casings), or simmer them until warmed through (if you used cellulose casings).

Serve with roasted red bell peppers, a drizzle of good olive oil, and a hunk of crusty bread.

MAKES 20 to 25 CHIPOLATA-SIZE SAUSAGES

10.5 ounces bacalao, filleted, chopped, and soaked in plenty of cold water overnight

1⅓ cups shallots, finely chopped

3 garlic cloves, finely chopped

5 tablespoons olive oil

1 ounce flat-leaf parsley, chopped

4 large eggs

2½ teaspoons ground Pimentón de la Vera, sweet

5.3 ounces crème fraîche or thick sour cream

1 pound 9 ounces potatoes, boiled until soft and drained

small spool of sheep casings or cellulose casings

2 teaspoons butter (optional)

MUSHROOM SAUSAGES WITH CAVOLO NERO & POTATOES

SERVES 4

The Sausages

1 pound 2 ounces white
mushrooms, 3.5 ounces shiitake
mushrooms, and 0.4 ounces dried
porcini powder

2 medium red onions, peeled

$\frac{1}{3}$ cup plus heaping 1 tablespoon
olive oil, plus extra for pan-frying

0.5 ounces garlic, finely chopped

1.8 ounces drained capers, chopped

5.3 ounces fresh white bread crumbs

3.5 ounces Parmesan cheese, shredded

1 teaspoon salt and 2½ teaspoons
freshly ground black pepper

1 ounce flat-leaf parsley, chopped

7 ounces crème fraîche or thick
sour cream

small spool of collagen or
cellulose casings

The Accompaniments

6 medium potatoes, unpeeled, diced

a few rosemary sprigs

1 pound 10 ounces cavolo nero

2 garlic cloves, chopped, and
2 dashes dried chile flakes

The luxurious sausages at the heart of this dish are flavored with three kinds of mushroom, including ground dried porcini, which imparts an earthy depth. They are best made with collagen or cellulose casings; these rupture easily in the frying pan, so blanch them.

Chop or blend the mushrooms and onions together until finely diced, then fry in the $\frac{1}{3}$ cup plus heaping 1 tablespoon olive oil, stirring frequently, until the juices have evaporated, about 30 minutes.

Transfer the mushroom and onion mixture to a large bowl and thoroughly mix in the rest of the ingredients.

Fill the stuffing into collagen casings and twist into about 20 sausages that are each around 6 inches long. Take care to tie them off well— given the slightest opportunity they will spurt out their contents.

Blanch the sausages in water heated to 176 to 185°F (any hotter and the casings will split) for 15 minutes. (If you don't plan to eat them immediately, cool them down under cold running water and store in the refrigerator for up to 5 days, or in the freezer for up to 4 months, then when you're ready to eat them, thaw if frozen and simmer for until warmed through, about 5 minutes.)

Meanwhile, boil the diced potatoes until soft, about 15 minutes. After draining, fry them with the rosemary in 3 tablespoons olive oil over medium heat, stirring frequently.

Remove the spines from the cavolo nero and discard. Coarsely chop the leaves. Stir-fry the cavolo nero with the garlic and chile flakes in enough oil to cover the bottom of a large pan or wok. The cabbage needs to be cooked hard for a few minutes and stirred vigorously until it has wilted.

Serve everything together on a large platter.

GLAMORGAN SAUSAGE WITH CREAMY BABY SPINACH

Purists might say that the Welsh Glamorgan sausage is no more sausage than Bombay Duck is duck or eggplant caviar the eggs of sturgeon. Never mind. These cheesy delights are well worth experimenting with. They can be pan-fried in butter or oil, or you can bake them. If you opt for the latter, drizzle a little oil over them before they go in the oven to help them cook evenly.

Put the cheese, half the bread crumbs, the leek, parsley, thyme, eggs, mustard, and half the cream into a large bowl. Season with the salt and white pepper, then roll up your sleeves and mix everything together.

Shape the mixture into small sausages and roll them in the remaining bread crumbs.

Gently fry the sausages in a small amount of olive oil until golden brown. Be careful with them, as they are fragile.

While the sausages are frying, pour a bit of olive oil into a large wok or pan and place over medium heat. Wilt the spinach, stirring continuously, then season with salt, pepper, and the nutmeg. Finally, stir in the remaining cream and serve alongside the piping hot sausages.

SERVES 4 to 6

The Sausages

9 ounces Caerphilly cheese or New York white cheddar, finely grated

7 ounces fresh white bread crumbs

½ medium leek, washed and finely chopped

2 tablespoons chopped flat-leaf parsley

1 thyme sprig, chopped

2 eggs

2 heaped teaspoons Dijon mustard

¾ cup plus heaping 1 tablespoon heavy cream

1 teaspoon salt

½ teaspoon ground white pepper

olive oil, for pan-frying

The Spinach

olive oil, for stir-frying

1 pound 2 ounces baby leaf spinach

salt and freshly ground black pepper

¼ nutmeg, freshly grated

FISHCAKE SAUSAGES

These charming little sausages are always a hit with small children. You can make them with most kinds of fish fillet. Haddock works well, as does salmon.

━━━━━━━━━━━━━━━━━━━━━━━━━━━━━━━━━━━

In a large bowl, thoroughly mash together all the ingredients except the casings. Don't be tempted to blend them in a food processor, as you want the sausages to have a bit of texture.

Fill the mixture into collagen casings and tie off into 6-inch links—you should have approximately 24 sausages.

Blanch the sausages in water heated to 176 to 185°F for 20 minutes (if you try to fry them they will burst).

Either serve the fishcake sausages immediately, perhaps accompanied by asparagus tips or peas, or cool them down under cold running water. They will keep in the refrigerator for up to 3 days or in the freezer for up to 4 months.

To reheat the sausages, simmer them gently in water heated to around 176°F for 10 minutes.

SERVES 4

1 pound 2 ounces skinless fish fillet, broken into small pieces

1 pound 2 ounces potatoes, peeled, sliced, and boiled for 20 minutes until soft

scant cup fresh white bread crumbs

½ cup plus 2 tablespoons heavy cream

2 eggs

½ cup drained capers, chopped

6 scallions, finely sliced

1 teaspoon salt

1¼ teaspoons ground white pepper

small spool of collagen casings

SAUSAGES A-Z

Andouille (France) Large sausages stuffed with, as well as encased by, various parts of the digestive tract of pigs, or less often veal. Often smoked, they are an acquired taste and sometimes stink to high heaven.

Andouille (U.S.) A heavily smoked pork and garlic sausage flavored with cayenne pepper. Used extensively in the Cajun cooking of Louisiana, for example in gumbos and jambalayas. Has none of the challenging features of French andouilles.

Andouillette Smaller version of andouille.

Bierwurst A precooked smoked German sausage made from beef and pork and flavored with garlic and mustard seed. A bit like salami in appearance. Doesn't contain beer, but goes very well with chilled lager.

Black pudding A British blood sausage containing a high proportion of oatmeal.

Bockwurst A Frankfurter-like sausage invented by R. Scholtz of Berlin in 1889. Usually smoked and flavored with paprika.

Boerwors The definitive South African sausage, made from coarsely cut pork, beef, or both. The name means "farmer's sausage." It is flavored with copious quantities of ground coriander and other spices, and contains vinegar.

Bologna A large smoked American sausage made of finely ground beef, pork, veal, or a mixture. Descended from the infinitely superior mortadella, it is known as "baloney" in some parts of the U.S., which indicates its low culinary status.

Boudin blanc A delectable precooked French sausage containing cream, eggs, and finely ground pork or chicken. Particularly popular around Christmas.

Boudin noir A cereal-free French blood sausage containing pork offal and head meat in addition to pig's blood.

Bratwurst A finely ground German sausage usually made from pork. The city of Nuremberg is famous for its bratwurst.

Butifarra A term covering a wide range of Catalan fresh pork sausages. Butifarra negra contains blood and mint as well as pork meat.

Cambridge An excellent fresh sausage from the English university town, spiced with nutmeg and sometimes ginger.

Cervelat The national sausage of Switzerland, made with emulsified pork and beef and lightly smoked. Also popular in Germany. The name comes from cervelle, the French for "brains," which used to be one of the key ingredients.

Chaurice Creole/Cajun version of chorizo.

Chipolata Small pork sausage, bizarrely deriving its name from "cipolla," the Italian for onion (it doesn't contain any).

Chorizo A family of Spanish and Latin American sausages whose common denominator is that they are made with pork and pimentón (paprika). Some are fresh, some cured. Mexican chorizo is particularly spicy, as it contains red chiles.

Chouriço Portuguese version of chorizo made with pork cured in brine.

Cotechino A fat (and fatty) pork-based Italian sausage traditionally eaten with lentils on New Year's Eve. Needs to be boiled before consumption.

Crepinette The French equivalent of a faggot, consisting of sausage meat wrapped in caul fat.

Cumberland A coarsely ground pork sausage traditionally formed into long, unbroken coils.

Drisheen Irish black pudding made with sheep's blood in Limerick, pig's blood in Cork and Kerry, and goose blood in Clare.

Extrawurst A German/Austrian precooked sausage made from beef, pork, or a combination of the two and usually eaten cold. The term "extrawurst" is also used of people with particularly high opinions of themselves.

Faggots British pork sausage meat packages wrapped in caul fat. They often but not always contain variety meats.

Figatello Corsican sausage made with lamb's liver.

Frankfurter Arguably the world's most popular sausage. Usually made with pork in Germany and beef in the U.S.

Fuet A thin pure pork salami from Catalunya, Spain. The name means "whip."

Gänseleberwurst A luxurious German sausage made from goose liver and truffles.

Garlic sausage In the U.K. at least, a large steam-cooked sausage made from cured pork, garlic, and spices. Usually sliced and eaten cold.

Glamorgan A Welsh vegetarian sausage made with Caerphilly cheese and encased in bread crumbs rather than a sausage casing.

Gloucester A fresh pork sausage flavored with sage and other herbs, traditionally made with meat from the Gloucester Old Spot pig.

Goteborg Hard smoked Swedish sausage made from beef and pork in a three to one ratio.

Gyulai Mildly smoked Hungarian sausage made with pork and bell peppers.

Haggis The "chieftain o' the puddin' race," traditionally made with sheep's lungs, liver, and spleen plus oatmeal and onions. Traditionally sown into a sheep's stomach, it is now usually stuffed into beef bungs.

Hammelwurst A German mutton sausage.

Jésus A huge French salami.

Kabanos A thin, smoked Polish sausage made from densely packed pork and often flavored with caraway seed.

Kielbasa In its native Polish, the word kielbasa just means "sausage." In the U.S., the term denotes a smoked precooked sausage made with pork, garlic, and marjoram.

Kindziuk/Skilandis Cold-smoked, pork-based Lithuanian sausage containing pure alcohol.

Knackwurst/Knockwurst A short, thick precooked German sausage made with beef, pork, or a mixture of both.

Knockpølse The Danish equivalent of knackwurst.

Kosher salami Made with beef rather than pork for obvious reasons.

Krakowska A lean, close-textured smoked Polish sausage originally from the city of Krakow.

Landjäger A square Swabian sausage made with beef, caraway, and garlic, and cold smoked.

Lap cheong A hard, air-dried Chinese pork sausage with a sweet flavor. The name literally means "waxed intestine."

Leberwurst Smooth, precooked, liver-based sausage from Germany. Pig's liver usually accounts for about 20 percent of its weight. The rest is made up of lean and fat pork, onions, and various spices.

Lincolnshire Coarsely ground fresh pork sausage flavored with sage.

Linguica Portuguese/Brazilian pork sausage made with garlic, paprika, and onion. Usually smoked and needs to be cooked before consumption.

Longaniza Spanish cured sausage similar to chorizo. Very popular in Latin America and the Philippines. The Argentinian version is flavored with anise seed.

Loukanika Fresh Greek pork or lamb sausage distinctively flavored with red wine and orange zest.

Lucanian Ancient Roman fresh pork sausage described by the fourth-century cookery writer Apicius. Key ingredients include crushed almonds and garum, a condiment made from fermented fish.

Mazzafegato Pork liver sausage from Norcia in Italy containing pine nuts, fennel, and garlic.

Medwurst Smoked, semi-dry pork sausage from Sweden containing potatoes.

Merguez Spicy red North African sausage made from lamb or beef, but never pork. Excellent with couscous.

Mettwurst Cold-smoked German sausage usually made from pure pork, but sometimes incorporating veal and/or beef. Some versions are soft and spreadable, others are harder.

Morcilla Spanish blood sausage made with cooked rice.

Mortadella Huge, classic precooked sausage from Bologna, Italy, made with finely ground pork and cubed fat in a ratio of seven to three. Sometimes studded with pistachio nuts and flavored with wine, it always contains garlic and is usually eaten in thin slices.

Newmarket Johnny's uncle would never speak to him again if we didn't include this excellent herby pork sausage from Suffolk. There are two versions, reflecting the fact that two different butchers claim possession of the "authentic" recipe. One contains bread crumbs, the other rusk.

Nham Fermented Thai pork sausage containing cooked rice, garlic, and fiery chiles.

Oyster sausage Very popular in Victorian times, oyster sausages contain veal or pork in addition to the bivalve that gives them their name.

Pepperoni Spelled "peperone" in its native Italy, this spicy, cured salami-like sausage is one of the world's favorite pizza toppings. It is made with a mixture of beef and pork, and gets its kick from hot red peppers.

Polish smoked Generic term for hot smoked pork sausages from guess where, Poland.

Reindyrpølse Norwegian reindeer sausage.

Rindswurst Precooked beef sausage from Frankfurt, which the locals tend to eat in greater quantities than the more famous pork sausage named after their city (see Germany feature, page 90).

Rookwurst A spicy Dutch smoked sausage featured in the "How to Smoke Sausages" section of the introductory chapter of this book.

Rosette A salami from the Lyon region of France.

Salami Any member of a vast family of fermented sausages made with raw meat distinctively interspersed with cubes of fatback. Some of the best-known varieties include:
Danish Bright pink variety made in enormous quantities for export. The Danes have been making salami since the Middle Ages.
Felino Pure pork plus wine and garlic
Finocchiona Made with fennel.
Fiorentino Usually made with pure pork and often includes larger pieces of lean meat among the fat and finely ground pork.
Hungarian, aka Pick Arguably the finest salami in the world, "Pick" is made from pure pork and is lightly smoked before a long period of curing. The salamis were originally made with donkey meat, but there weren't enough donkeys in the country to meet demand.
Milanese A finely textured salami made with pork and beef or veal flavored with garlic and whole white peppercorns.
Napolitano A feisty pork-and-beef-based salami flavored with hot red peppers.
Nola Unlike most Italian salamis, this variety is smoked.

Salchichas Fresh Spanish sausages.

Salchichon de Vic A kind of cross between salami and cured chorizo made in the Catalunyan city of Vic in Spain.

Salsiccie Robust fresh Italian pork sausages.

Saucisse Fresh French sausages, available in almost infinite varieties.

Saucisson Cured French sausages. The most famous is probably saucisson sec, which is a simple, quick-cured salami made from pure pork.

Saveloy A bright red emulsified sausage sold from the counters of British "fish and chip" shops.

Schinkenwurst/Shinkenplockwurst Smoked sausage made in Westphalia in Germany from flaked ham studded with largish cubes of fatback.

Sheftalia Cypriot pork or lamb sausage flavored with parsley and onion and wrapped in caul fat. For maximum authenticity and flavor, sheftalia should be grilled.

Soppressata A variety of salami made in the Southern Italian provinces of Calabria, Puglia, and Basilicato. Usually pressed flat during the maturing phase and heavily flavored with garlic.

Sucuk Lean fermented beef and lamb sausage from Turkey.

Summer sausage Fermented, salami-style sausage from the U.S. Usually made from a mixture of pork and beef, it is often smoked. It derives its name from the fact that it is ready to eat in the summer, not because it is made in that season. It is traditionally made in the fall.

Teewurst Soft, spreadable, uncooked German sausage made from two parts pork and or beef and one part bacon fat. After being stuffed into casings, the sausages are smoked over beechwood and hung to mature for a week to ten days. Teewurst derives its name from the fact that it is traditionally consumed at tea time.

Thuringer Fresh grilling sausage from the German state of Thuringia, made with finely ground meat flavored with garlic, caraway, and marjoram. By law, German fresh sausages must be sold on the day they are made.

Toulouse A coarse fresh sausage from South West France made with pork belly, red wine, garlic, and nutmeg. Toulouse sausages are an essential ingredient in cassoulet.

Weisswurst Emulsified Bavarian sausage made from finely ground veal or pork and flavored with parsley. Weisswurst are highly perishable. Residents of Munich have a phobia about eating them after the noon bells chime.

White pudding British sausage usually based on shredded pork or chicken and invariably containing oatmeal and suet. Fried slices of white pudding are an integral part of a proper Irish breakfast. Scottish white pudding, also known as mealy pudding, sometimes doesn't contain any meat at all.

Wiejska A lightly smoked, precooked Polish sausage. Wiejska means "rural."

Wienerwurst Alternative name for Frankfurter, often corrupted to "Wienie" in the U.S.

Zampone Similar to a Cotechino, but with the distinctive feature of being encased in a boned-out pig's hock.

INDEX